Thanksgiving

Thanksgiving

Unit Study Guide to the
Pilgrims and Their Faith

Amanda Bennett

AABennett Books

**For updates and more information,
check out the
"And What About . . ." series website at
www.andwhatabout.com**

OTHER BOOKS BY THIS AUTHOR:
**A Unit Study Journal
Christmas
Patriotic Holidays
Lighthouses
Sailing Ships
. . . and more to come**

Published by AABennett Books, P.O. Box 1777, Dunlap, Tennessee 37327.

Library of Congress Card Number: 2001118354

Printed in the United States of America
1 2 3 4 5 6 7 8 —05 04 03 02 01

"Be careful for nothing; but in every thing by
prayer and supplication
with thanksgiving
let your requests be made known unto God."

— *Philippians 4:6*

TABLE OF CONTENTS

Unit Studies The Easy Way!

Welcome to the new **"And What About"** series—easy-to-use unit studies written in a cross-curricular approach about many interesting and important topics. Using simplicity and readily-available resources to enhance the learning process, your children can learn about these topics in ways never before possible. Unit studies allow students to use a natural learning process—one that is so familiar to us as we become adults, and yet is far removed from textbooks, which are full of concentrated and condensed facts and figures.

Using these studies, your children will learn about a particular topic, covering the science, history, geography, art, and any other areas of study that apply to the topic. For example, while working on **Thanksgiving**, they will discover the important role of faith and freedom in American history. They will learn how desperate the pilgrims were to find freedom from persecution and how they learned to work together as a team, something which was not always easy for a mixture of "Saints" and "Strangers"!

These books make learning a fascinating and thought-provoking adventure, which is the way that learning SHOULD be—life-long learners are successful, inquisitive, and engaging, contributing so much to our world. Let's face it—many people would love to give up their dry and fact-filled textbooks to try unit studies, but they don't have the time to do the research and/or preparation, or they lack the confidence to try a new method of learning.

I understand these difficulties and hesitations all too well. As we considered educating our own children using unit studies, we had the same questions. Where do we begin; how do I structure the study; what do I cover; how do I record the work? This series of books is a product of this adventure—**designed to make your path simpler and your load lighter, while guiding your students along a successful road of learning.**

Written with you and your family in mind, you will know what to do each day; what to cover; and what is important about this topic. The research and preparation have been done for you. The

daily plan and assignments are here, ready for immediate use. You will find that these guides use the Internet as a primary resource. This has been done for many reasons, among which include the wealth of information now available online for in-depth studies, the ease of accessing this information for most parents and teachers, as well as the fact that it is affordable and much simpler to use than numerous trips to the library or bookstore.

The Internet sites have been carefully screened for appropriate content for the study. From virtual tours to fun projects that are EASY to make, the wealth of information is amazing. We will visit a replica of the *Mayflower* and learn more about the Pilgrims' journey aboard the ship. We will read about Captain John Smith and his contribution to the settlement of New England. Using the Internet, we can visit Plimoth Plantation and take a virtual tour of the plantation and discover how the Wamponoag lived. You will get a better feel for how primitively the Pilgrims lived, walk their fields of promise, and understand how their dream was realized—things that we would not be able to see with our "book" encyclopedias. We can even learn to make some of the foods that they prepared at their first harvest festival.

This book is divided into four weeks of study—one for each major topic of the Thanksgiving study. The first page of each week has a list of the OBJECTIVES for that week. Designed for all ages from early elementary through adult, each day has a basic structured learning plan for ELEMENTARY GRADES and one for JR/SR HIGH.

The Learning Plan for each day of the week is comprised of the following basic daily components:

- TODAY'S QUOTE—to be read, copied, and perhaps even memorized.
- WORDS OF WISDOM (WOW)—spelling/vocabulary words and their definitions to be written, studied, and learned.
- INTERESTING PEOPLE AND PLACES—Important and interesting people and places will be investigated during the study
- READ AND DISCOVER—questions that must be researched and answered as each topic is explored.

UNIT STUDIES—THE EASY WAY!

<u>Ready to Begin the Easy Way of Using Unit Studies? Here We Go!</u>

1. Take a few minutes to look through the study and the list of Favorite Books included in the introduction section of this book. Do you already have some of the titles in your family library? Note some of the books that you think might be interesting and request them from the library for this study.

2. With the growth of available online information, we have made extensive use of many of the Internet sites that work well with this study. These sites have been carefully chosen for their content, but site content can change in a moment, so parents/teachers should visit the sites first as you begin the day's study. Should you find a site that isn't working, visit our web page at www.andwhatabout.com/sites to find updates for these listings.

3. Pick up an inexpensive spiral notebook, report folder, or composition notebook for each student, to be used as their Thanksgiving Journal. They can decorate the notebook or folder with Pilgrims, ships, and Thanskgiving designs, stickers, and decorations.

4. Collect some materials for a Family Thanksgiving Memories Album. This album is going to include a collection of your family memories of this study—photos of the projects and papers, as well as any souvenirs that your family collects along the way. You can use a three-ring binder and notebook paper, or a scrapbook or regular photo album. Use this album, year after year, to record your further Thanksgiving studies, memories, menus, and photographs—create a treasure!

5. Look over the FAMILY PROJECTS page, located on page 9. Keep some of these in mind for each week of the study, using them as they fit into your family's studies and schedule.

Now, take off and enjoy the adventure—there is much to be learned, and it should be fun for everyone. Before I forget—realize that your students may take off on new tangents that pertain to the topic, but you will be able to maintain the basic flow of learning using this unit study guide. Remember, life-long learners have plenty of ground to cover!

Happy Thanksgiving, and may God bless you and your family abundantly!
Amanda

"It cannot be emphasized too strongly
or too often that this great nation was founded,
not by religionists, but by Christians;
not on religions,
but on the gospel of Jesus Christ!
For this very reason,
peoples of other faiths have been afforded
asylum, prosperity,
and freedom to worship here."

— Patrick Henry

Introduction

Thanksgiving is a time of gratitude, thankfulness, and counting God's blessings, while we enjoy a bountiful feast with friends and family around us. Thanksgiving has become an American holiday that encompasses many special traditions and historical events. From the baking of the pumpkin pie and the roasting of the turkey to the glad shouts of arriving friends and family and the smiles on everyone's faces—these are the familiar sights, sounds, and smells that remind us of this special day and its significance. We have so much to be thankful for, and this special day is one during which we choose to show our thanks and share our bounty and blessings with those that we hold dear.

From the very first harvest celebration of the Pilgrims, the later celebration of Forefathers' Day, and the need to give thanks for all that we Americans have been blessed with, Thanksgiving has evolved into a uniquely American holiday. With such a rich history of the early colonization of this country, the story of the Saints and Strangers unfolds like a good novel, vividly holding our interest. Far different than the dry brief history that we were taught as children, this part of history has been interesting for all of us, adults and children alike, to study.

The story of these people, their plight, and the time span and geography covered, is amazing to learn about. The Pilgrim's endurance and commitment, their willingness to leave the known and comfortable to go to the unknown, and their hard work and deep faith in God helped them firmly establish themselves in the New World. At the same time, Europeans were already interacting with Native Americans along North American shores. Captain John Smith had already explored the New England area and a small area that Prince Charles had named "Plymouth"—soon to be settled by the Pilgrims. Stories about the various tribes and their members such as Squanto and Samoset have touched us, along with their willingness to help the Pilgrims survive by sharing their knowledge of farming and hunting.

I hope you enjoy the journey into this portion of America's past. Without the prayerful thought and religious consideration of the Pilgrims in writing the Mayflower Compact, we probably would not enjoy the religious freedom that we have come to expect and appreciate. At our house, we choose to celebrate this holiday by showing our thanks for God's providence and grace. May you and your family enjoy this study as you turn back the pages of time with us, enjoying the learning and counting your blessings along the way! Happy Thanksgiving, and may God richly bless you and yours!

A SPECIAL NOTE

Even though every effort is made to thoroughly research each website listed, sites do change, and content as well as access can change at any moment. If you find a website suggestion in this guide that no longer works, please let me know at **amanda@andwhatabout.com**. We will be frequently updating these site listings on our webpage, **www.andwhatabout.com/sites** as necessary.

In the meantime, if you need to locate other sites for your study, these are my favorite search engines:

SEARCH ENGINES THAT ARE PROMOTED AS BEING FOR KIDS:

(I always recommend that an adult check the search results first, then share appropriate sites with their students)
- www.yahooligans.com
- http://lycoszone.lycos.com

SEARCH ENGINES THAT I USE FOR MY OWN UNIT STUDY RESEARCH:
- www.google.com

(Click on the Advanced Search button on the main page. On the next page, fill in the search fields making SURE to also select to turn ON Safe Filter!)
- www.lycos.com

(WITH the parental controls turned ON—look in the upper right hand corner of screen)

Favorite Books

Here are some of the books that complement this unit study. You don't need them all—just try to find a few that sound interesting for your students. As society moves toward a more "politically correct" representation of history, accurate books about our forefathers and their adventures are becoming fewer in number. Good luck in your adventures, and check our website, **www.andwhatabout.com**, from time to time. Click on the Thanksgiving link to find out if there are new book recommendations or web site suggestions!

Family Read-Alouds

Here are some of my suggestions for family reading when studying Thanksgiving, and this first book is my top recommendation for any study of the Pilgrims!

William Bradford: Plymouth's Faithful Pilgrim, by Gary D. Schmidt. Published by Eerdman's Books for Young Readers. A terrific book for the family, particularly for ages 10 and up. The author carefully walks the reader through the childhood, developing faith, and experiences of William Bradford. The book brings together the details of the Separatists—their emigration from England to the Netherlands and then to the New World. The artwork, maps, and photos add depth and unforgettable meaning to the story of this man and his work to establish a vital colony. HIGHLY RECOMMENDED!

My Name is America: The Journal of Jasper Pierce, A Pilgrim Boy, 1620, by Ann Rinaldi. Published by Scholastic. A story of the Pilgrims journey and their new life as seen through the eyes of a boy who is an indentured servant (fiction). The author shows the reader the trials and triumphs, fears and adventures that the Pilgrims experienced during that first year. Ages 10 and up.

A Journey to the New World: The Diary of Remember Patience Whipple, Mayflower 1620 (Dear America), by Kathryn Lasky. Published by Scholastic Trade. This story is a fictional account of a twelve-year-old girl and her journey to the New World,

Thanksgiving

as seen from her diary entries. This book does describe the very real hardships of the Pilgrims, and her mother dies the first winter at Plymouth. It is a story of courage, trials, and perseverance. Ages 10 and up.

Squanto and the Miracle of Thanksgiving, by Eric Metaxas. Published by Tommy Nelson. What an uplifting and fascinating historical story—showing the readers that the real hero of the Pilgrim's first thanksgiving celebration was God! Ages 5 and up.

The Pilgrims at Plymouth, by Lucille Recht Penner. (Picture Landmark Books). Published by Random House. Describes the voyage and settlement of Plymouth with plenty of interesting illustrations. This book begins with the departure of the *Mayflower*—it doesn't explain much of why the Pilgrims made their voyage. Ages 5 and up.

Pilgrim's Progress, by John Bunyan, edited by Edward Hazelbaker. Published by Bridge-Logos Publishers. The study of the American Pilgrims provides a wonderful opportunity to read *Pilgrim's Progress*. This edition is one that is written in modern English and is reader-friendly, while also providing Bunyan's annotations in the text. Ages 10 and up.

General Family Interest

N.C. Wyeth's Pilgrims, illustrated by N.C. Wyeth and text by Robert D. San Souci. Published by Chronicle Books. The artwork of N.C. Wyeth is interesting! Even though quite romanticized, these paintings will draw the reader into the story of the Pilgrims. Ages 8 and up.

Eating The Plates: A Pilgrim Book of Food and Manners, by Lucille Recht Penner. Published by Aladdin Paperbacks. Learn all about the table manners (not many!), food, and cooking of the Pilgrims. There are recipes that your family can cook together, providing a first-hand appreciation of the spices and foods that we take for granted these days. Ages 6 and up.

Favorite Books

Cut and Assemble the Mayflower, from Dover Publications. The model of the *Mayflower* is cut from the pages of this book and glued together—great for the whole family and for use as a centerpiece. Ages 10 and up.

Younger Students

Samuel Eaton's Day: A Day in the Life of a Pilgrim Boy, by Kate Waters. Published by Scholastic Trade. This book tells the story of a day in the life of seven-year-old Samuel Eaton. The story describes his family, his responsibilities, and his play at Plymouth, using photos taken at Plimoth Plantation. Ages 4 and up.

Sarah Morton's Day: A Day in the Life of a Pilgrim Girl, by Kate Waters. Published by Scholastic Trade. Like *Samuel Eaton's Day,* this book tells the story of a day in the life of Sarah Morton—her family, responsibilities, and education at home, using photographs taken at Plimoth Plantation. Ages 4 and up.

On The Mayflower: Voyage of the Ship's Apprentice and a Passenger Girl, by Kate Waters. Published by Scholastic Trade. Written from the perspective of the young ship's apprentice, this book tells the story of what life might have been like for young people onboard the *Mayflower.* Using photos taken on the *Mayflower II,* the book helps the reader to see what conditions were like during their journey. Ages 4 and up.

Tapenum's Day: A Wampanoag Indian Boy in Pilgrim Times, by Kate Waters. Published by Scholastic Trade. Like *Samuel Eaton's Day* and *Sarah Morton's Day,* the author describes the daily life of a Wampanoag boy during the time of the Pilgrims. The photos are taken of a modern Wampanoag boy at the Plimoth Plantation historical site. Ages 9 and up.

If You Sailed on the Mayflower in 1620, by Ann McGovern. Published by Scholastic Trade. Written in a question and answer format, this delightful book keeps readers busy with all kinds of information about the Pilgrims and their journey—perfect for the inquisitive child filled with questions! Ages 5 and up.

Thanksgiving

Three Young Pilgrims, by Cheryl Harness. Published by Aladdin Paperbacks. This book is a fictionalized account of the Allerton family—their voyage in the *Mayflower*, their difficult first winter, and the harvest of the next year. Well-illustrated, the book reminds the reader that the Pilgrims were made up of families with children, just like their own. Ages 6 and up.

Squanto and the Miracle of Thanksgiving, by Eric Metaxas. Published by Tommy Nelson. What an uplifting and fascinating historical story—showing the readers that the real hero of the Pilgrim's first thanksgiving celebration was God! Ages 5 and up.

The Pilgrims at Plymouth, by Lucille Recht Penner. (Picture Landmark Books). Published by Random House. Describes the voyage and settlement of Plymouth with plenty of interesting illustrations. This book begins with the departure of the *Mayflower*—it doesn't explain much of why the Pilgrims made their voyage. Ages 5 and up.

The Pilgrim's First Thanksgiving, by Ann McGovern. Published by Scholastic Trade. Well-illustrated story of the first thanksgiving, or harvest festival, that the Pilgrims celebrated in 1621. Ages 5 and up.

Goody O'Grumpity, by Carol Ryrie Brink. Published by North-South Books. A fun book to read, and then you can bake the spice cake that Goody O'Grumpity bakes for hungry children. The story of Goody O'Grumpity was written in a 1937 poem by Carol Ryrie Brink. The illustrator researched the poem, and her research led to Plimoth Plantation! Ages 4 and up.

Cranberry Thanksgiving, by Wende and Harry Devlin. Published by Aladdin Paperbacks. A mystery to solve, Thanksgiving dinner, and a recipe for Cranberry bread—all included in this classic holiday tale for the whole family. Like *Goody O'Grumpity*, this book will have your family in the kitchen again! Ages 4 and up.

Favorite Books

American Family of Pilgrim Paper Dolls, by Tom Tierney. Published by Dover Publications. Fun projects for ages 6 to 10.

More Than Moccasins: A Kid's Activity Guide to Traditional North American Indian Life, by Laurie Carlson. Published by Chicago Review Press. Full of activities, recipes, and simple-to-do projects, this book is also full of history and information. Ages 5 to 10.

Older Students

The Landing of the Pilgrims, by James Daugherty. Published by Random House. One of the Landmark series, this book provides the reader with a readable and accurate account of the Pilgrims' efforts to settle Plymouth. Ages 11 and up.

Mourt's Relation: A Journal of the Pilgrims at Plymouth, by William Bradford. Originally printed in 1622, this book describes the adventures of the Pilgrims from their voyage through the early years at Plymouth. Ages 14 and up.

Good Newes From New England, by Edward Winslow. First published in 1642, this book was probably written to persuade other English families to come join the Pilgrims in the New World.

Faith Unfurled: The Pilgrim's Quest for Freedom, edited by Sheila Foley. Published by Discovery Enterprises. A valuable collection of journal entries, poetry, and other resource material that provides insight about the determination and faith of the Pilgrims. Ages 13 and up.

Three Visitors To Early Plymouth, published by Applewood Books. This book contains the letters of three young men that visited early Plymouth at different times (1622, 1624, and 1628). They describe the colony and their impressions during their visits. Ages 14 and up.

Thanksgiving

The World of Captain John Smith, by Genevieve Foster. Republished by Beautiful Feet Books. Mrs. Foster did an excellent job of using words to show the reader a horizontal slice of life at a point in time. In this book, she describes what the world was like during the life of Captain Smith — the religious, cultural, social, and economic conditions around the world. Some of the topics include Shakespeare, Galileo, and Mary Queen of Scots. Well illustrated by the author. Ages 12 and up.

Land Ho! 1620: A Seaman's Story of the Mayflower, Her Construction, Her Navigation, and Her First Landfall, by W. Sears Nickerson. Published by Michigan State University Press. For those interested in the *Mayflower* and sailing ships, this book has been written by an expert in sailing and navigation. Using tide and sunrise tables, along with other information, the author traces the voyage of the *Mayflower* to the New World. Ages 14 and up.

Pilgrim's Progress, by John Bunyan, edited by Edward Hazelbaker. Published by Bridge-Logos Publishers. The study of the American Pilgrims provides a wonderful opportunity for older students to read *Pilgrim's Progress*. This edition is one that is written in modern English and is reader-friendly, while also providing Bunyan's annotations in the text. Ages 10 and up.

Family Projects

1. Visit a local farm for a tour of the facilities and try to observe a crop being harvested. Check your local newspaper for seasonal farm tours and self-pick farms that your family might enjoy visiting. There are local pumpkin farms, apple orchards, and many others that can be fun to visit and tour. We've taken hayrides, walked fields of pumpkins as far as the eye can see, picked apples, and watched the making of apple cider and apple butter. This helps everyone understand and appreciate just what goes into a harvest and enjoy the fruits of the harvest together!

2. Many Native American festivals are held throughout the autumn months. Attending one of these festivals can provide a fun learning experience—seeing the native dress, food, housing, and handwork of Native American tribes. Check your local newspaper for listings, as well as regional magazines that list community events (Southern Living, Yankee, etc.).

3. If you live in the Northeast or are planning a vacation to the Massachusetts area, consider visiting Plimoth Plantation, a living history museum where the settlement has been reconstructed and a full-scale reproduction of the *Mayflower* can be seen. Interpreters explain their daily chores and answer visitors' questions, as they work through the daily routines of life in Plimoth Colony in 1627. There is a reconstruction of a Wampanoag Indian homesite to visit as well.

4. Another Thanksgiving tradition that the whole family can enjoy is the construction of a "Blessing Tree." When beginning this unit, work together to construct a brown tree trunk from brown paper (several feet tall—ours is about four-feet tall and two-feet wide with a few bare branches) to be hung on a door. Then, using several different colors of construction paper, have everyone cut out 30 life-size leaves each—these are called our "blessing leaves." The tree trunk is taped or attached to the door, and everyone glues a new leaf to the paper tree daily after writing something that he or she is thankful for on the leaf! I have saved some of our most precious blessing leaves in our Thanksgiving Album, and we've accumulated some real gems! By the time Thanksgiving Day approaches, the branches of the tree are

beautifully filled out with a show of many autumn colors. All of the family, friends, and neighbors that come to visit will enjoy reading the sentiments as much as you and your family do! Don't forget to take a picture of your Blessings Tree.

5. Build a model of the *Mayflower*, either a commercially prepared model or build your own using construction blocks, craft sticks, or modeling clay. Use a picture of the *Mayflower* in one of the Thanksgiving books or from the **www.plimoth.org** website.

6. Using modeling clay and a diagram of Plimoth Plantation, spend some time with your family creating your own model of the Pilgrims' colony. This can be as detailed as you would like, and everyone can work at their own level of interest—the final product will be quite a creation! You can construct your colony on a piece of poster paper, a cookie sheet, or perhaps a sheet of wax paper. It makes quite a table centerpiece for Thanksgiving Day. Don't forget to take pictures along the way for your Thanksgiving memory album!

7. During the month, identify special people that could use a blessing—perhaps a batch of cookies, a loaf of banana bread, having their lawn raked, or an invitation to join your family for an evening meal. Once you've all contributed to this special list of people, work together to agree on how you would like to bless them. Then, using a calendar, assign one or two names to each Friday of November, and work through the week on their blessings!

8. Develop a Thanksgiving plan! Why not work together as a family this year, developing the plan together ahead of time. Fix the total budget first, then begin to plan the menu and match it carefully to the budgeted amount. This is an excellent project for students that are learning about budgets and meal planning! Next, work together to plan the day's festivities and the people that you would all like to invite. Spend an evening making invitations and souvenir menus for your guests. Assign the various steps of preparation to different family members, so that everyone helps and everyone gets to enjoy this special day together.

Thanksgiving
Week One

This week will be used to focus on the background history of the Pilgrims.

Objectives

- Define the word "thanksgiving" and explore what it means to be thankful
- Discover what the Reformation was and how it impacted the churchgoers of England
- Find out who the Separatists were and why they had to leave England
- Learn about the Pilgrim's immigration to Holland — where they went and what they discovered there

Thanksgiving

WEEK ONE: Day One

As we begin our study of Thanksgiving, we are going to take today to think about what thanksgiving means and what the holiday means to your family.

Elementary Grades

TODAY'S QUOTE: Copy today's quote into your Thanksgiving Journal:
"Enter into his gates with thanksgiving, and into his courts with praise: be thankful unto him, and bless his name."

—Psalm 100:4

WOW: Look up the following words in the dictionary and write the words and their definitions in your Thanksgiving Journal:
1. thanks
2. giving
3. pray
4. feast

INTERESTING PEOPLE & PLACES: Using an encyclopedia or Internet site, look up **King David.** Who was he, and where in the Bible can you find some of his writing? Write or narrate a paragraph about King David in your Thanksgiving Journal.

READ AND DISCOVER: Using an encyclopedia, dictionary, book, or Internet site, read the following questions and find the answers. Write or narrate your answers for your Journal.
1. What is meant by the word "thanksgiving"? Look the word up in a dictionary and write the definition in your Journal.
2. Why do you think we celebrate Thanksgiving? Describe your top two reasons in your Journal.
3. What does your family do to celebrate this holiday? Write or narrate a story about Thanksgiving at your house, including your favorite parts of the celebration!

RESOURCE: DICTIONARY.COM—visit this online dictionary to look up words in several different dictionaries.
http://www.dictionary.com

Week One

Junior/Senior High

TODAY'S QUOTE: Copy today's quote into your Thanksgiving Journal:
"Not what we say about our blessings, but how we use them, is the true measure of our thanksgiving."

— W.T. Purkiser

WOW: Look up the following words in the dictionary and write the words and their definitions in your Thanksgiving Journal:
1. Thanksgiving
2. blessings
3. celebrate
4. harvest

INTERESTING PEOPLE & PLACES: Using your Bible, an encyclopedia, or Internet site, look up **King David.** Who was he? Some of the most beautiful words of praise in the Bible were written by him. Where in the Bible can we find his writings? Summarize your answer in a paragraph in your Journal. Web site suggestion:
http://www.mustardseed.net/html/pedavid.html

READ AND DISCOVER: Using library books, encyclopedias, or Internet sites, find the answer to these questions and record your answers in your Journal along with the source of your information (book, encyclopedia, website, etc).
1. What is meant by the word "thanksgiving" — the word itself, not the holiday! Look it up, then write a description in your Journal.
2. How does your family celebrate Thanksgiving? Write at least two paragraphs that describe your favorite Thanksgiving holiday memory.
3. Write a letter to Plimoth Plantation, requesting information about the museum facility and the activities that will take place this coming Thanksgiving. Their address is: Plimoth Plantation, P.O. Box 1620, Plymouth, MA 02362

RESOURCE: DICTIONARY.COM — visit this online dictionary to look up words in several different dictionaries.
http://www.dictionary.com

Thanksgiving

WEEK ONE: Day Two

Today we are going to study the Reformation, learning more about what it was and how it impacted the lives of the people that we call "Pilgrims."

Elementary Grades

TODAY'S QUOTE: Copy today's quote into your Thanksgiving Journal:
"In every thing give thanks: for this is the will of God in Christ Jesus concerning you."   —1 Thessalonians 5:18

WOW: Look up the following words in the dictionary and write the words and their definitions in your Thanksgiving Journal:
  1. blessing
  2. faith
  3. hope
  4. give

INTERESTING PEOPLE & PLACES: Using an encyclopedia, globe, or Internet site, look up **England.** Can you find **Plymouth, England**? Draw a map of England in your Journal, marking Plymouth on the map. Website:
  http://school.discovery.com/homeworkhelp/worldbook/
    atozpictures/mp001112.html

READ AND DISCOVER: Using an book or website, read the following questions and find the answers. Write your answers in your Journal.
  1. What was the Reformation? Website suggestion:
  http://school.discovery.com/homeworkhelp/worldbook/
    atozhistory/r/463180.html
  2. One of the people that began to reform the church was Martin Luther. He had studied the Bible, and he was unhappy with some of the things that were happening within the Catholic Church. Look up Martin Luther to see what you can find out about him. When did he live, and what did he do to protest against some things the church was doing? Website suggestion:
  http://encarta.msn.com/find/Concise.asp?z=1&pg=2&ti=761570003

RESOURCE: PINE CONE TURKEY—CRAFT PROJECT
  http://www.kidsdomain.com/craft/turkey.html

Week One

Junior/Senior High

TODAY'S QUOTE: Copy today's quote into your Thanksgiving Journal: "Feeling gratitude and not expressing it is like wrapping a present and not giving it."
—William Arthur Ward

WOW: Look up the following words in the dictionary and write the words and their definitions in your Thanksgiving Journal:
1. suffer
2. beliefs
3. worship
4. grateful

INTERESTING PEOPLE & PLACES: Using an encyclopedia, atlas, or Internet site, find **England.** In England, locate the towns of **Scrooby, Boston,** and **Plymouth.** What do each of these towns have to do with the Pilgrims? Summarize your answer in your Journal.

READ AND DISCOVER: Using library books, encyclopedias, or Internet sites, find the answer to these questions and record your answers in your Journal along with the source of your information (book, encyclopedia, web site, etc).

1. Just exactly what is meant when we talk about the "Reformation?" When did it occur, and what effect did it have on the people of Europe? Summarize your answer in two paragraphs in your Journal. Website suggestions:

http://encarta.msn.com/find/Concise.asp?z=1&pg=2&ti=761562628
http://elane.stanford.edu/wilson/Text/3c.html

2. Who was Martin Luther and what act of protest did he make that became famous throughout Europe? In your Journal, write a brief biography about him and include a description of his protest. Website suggestions:

http://encarta.msn.com/find/Concise.asp?z=1&pg=2&ti=761570003
http://www.gospelcom.net/chi/GLIMPSEF/Glimpses/glmps015.shtml

RESOURCES: BOSTON, LINCOLNSHIRE, ENGLAND
http://www.oedgs.com/city_boston_england.htm
THE REFORMATION AND SCOTLAND
http://www.bbc.co.uk/history/scottishhistory/renaissance/
features_renaissance_reformation.shtml

Thanksgiving

WEEK ONE: Day Three

This day will be spent learning about the Separatists, discovering who they were, what they believed, and why they had to leave England.

Elementary Grades

TODAY'S QUOTE: Copy today's quote into your Thanksgiving Journal: "There is always something for which to be thankful."

—Charles Dickens

WOW: Look up the following words in the dictionary and write the words and their definitions in your Thanksgiving Journal:
1. free
2. sail
3. ship
4. different

INTERESTING PEOPLE & PLACES: Using an encyclopedia or Internet site, look up **William Brewster.** Who was he, and why was he important? Write or narrate a paragraph about William Brewster in your Journal. Website suggestion:

> http://school.discovery.com/homeworkhelp/worldbook/ atozhistory/b/076060.html

READ AND DISCOVER: Using an encyclopedia, book, or Internet site, read the following questions and find the answers. Write or narrate your answers for your Journal.

1. Who were the Separatists? Why were they called "Separatists"? Who was one of their leaders? Website suggestion:

> http://www.pilgrimhall.org/whopilg.htm

2. King James ruled that all private religious meetings were against the law and that everyone had to attend **ONLY** the Church of England! How would you feel if someone forced you to attend a government church?

RESOURCES:
ORIGINS OF THE SEPARATISTS
> http://kids.infoplease.lycos.com/ce6/history/A0860390.html

WILLIAM BREWSTER
> http://members.aol.com/calebj/brewster.html

Week One

<u>Junior/Senior High</u>

TODAY'S QUOTE: Copy today's quote into your Thanksgiving Journal: "Seeing our Father in everything makes life one long thanksgiving and gives rest of the heart."   —Hannah Whithall-Smith

WOW: Look up the following words in the dictionary and write the words and their definitions in your Thanksgiving Journal:
1. **differences**
2. **separate**
3. **purify**
4. **congregate**

INTERESTING PEOPLE & PLACES: Using an encyclopedia or Internet site, look up **William Brewster.** Who was he, and what did he have to do with the Separatists? Summarize your answer in a paragraph in your Journal. Website suggestions:

    http://kids.infoplease.lycos.com/ce6/people/A0808885.html

    http://school.discovery.com/homeworkhelp/worldbook/
      atozhistory/b/076060.html

READ AND DISCOVER: Using library books, encyclopedias, or Internet sites, find the answer to these questions and record your answers in your Journal along with the source of your information (book, encyclopedia, website, etc).

    1. Who were the Separatists, and where did their church form? What were the names of two of their original leaders? Websites:

    http://www.pilgrimhall.org/whopilg.htm

    http://www.plimoth.org/Library/scrooby.htm

    2. What do we know about their religious beliefs? How did they differ from the Church of England—which sacraments, holidays, and other topics varied from the English church? Website suggestion:

    http://members.aol.com/calebj/mayflower.html

    3. Write a letter to the Plymouth Visitor Information Center, requesting information about Plymouth and the activities that will take place this coming Thanksgiving. Their address is: Plymouth Visitor Information, P.O. Box ROCK, Plymouth, MA 02361.

RESOURCE: FREEDOM TRAIL—ROAD TO AMERICAN INDEPENDENCE
    http://www.bostonuk.com/historical/trail.htm

Thanksgiving

WEEK ONE: Day Four

Today we will investigate the immigration of the Separatists to Holland—where did they go and what did they discover there?

Elementary Grades

TODAY'S QUOTE: Copy today's quote into your Thanksgiving Journal:
"Now faith is the substance of things hoped for, the evidence of things not seen."
—Hebrews 11:1

WOW: Look up the following words in the dictionary and write the words and their definitions in your Thanksgiving Journal:
1. pilgrim
2. hide
3. flee
4. learn

INTERESTING PEOPLE & PLACES: We are going to learn more about the country that used to be called Holland, which is now considered the Netherlands. Using an encyclopedia, map, or Internet site, find the **Netherlands.** Can you see locate the town of **Leiden**? Draw a map of the Netherlands in your Journal. Website suggestion (at this site, read the first paragraph of the article, then click on the small map to go to a larger map that is easier to use):
> http://school.discovery.com/homeworkhelp/worldbook/
> atozgeography/n/387300.html

READ AND DISCOVER: Using an encyclopedia, book, or Internet site, read the following questions and find the answers. Write your answers in your Journal.
1. To avoid arrest, the Separatists had to move away from England. They moved to Leiden, Holland and stayed there until they decided to travel to the New World. How long did they live in Holland? Website suggestion:
> http://school.discovery.com/homeworkhelp/worldbook/
> atozhistory/p/430295.html

2. There was a famous artist in this same town, and his name was Rembrandt. Look him up in a book or online and look at some of his paintings. What was his full name? What year was he born, and how old was he when the Pilgrims sailed to America? Find one of his paintings and describe what you see in the painting. Website suggestion:
> http://sunsite.dk/cgfa/rembrand/rembrandt_bio.htm
> http://sunsite.dk/cgfa/rembrand/index.html

Week One

Junior/Senior High

TODAY'S QUOTE: Copy today's quote into your Thanksgiving Journal:
"One who has a faith which is not to be shaken has won it through blood and tears—has worked his or her way from doubt to truth as one who reaches a clearing through a thicket of brambles and thorns."

—Helen Keller

WOW: Look up the following words in the dictionary and write the words and their definitions in your Thanksgiving Journal:
1. refugee
2. pilgrim
3. religious
4. persecution

INTERESTING PEOPLE & PLACES: Using an atlas, encyclopedia, or Internet site, try to find **Holland**. That part of Europe is now know by another name—what is it? Where is **Leiden**? Summarize your answer in a paragraph in your Journal. Website suggestion (at this site, read the article, then click on the small map to go to a larger map that is easier to use):
> http://school.discovery.com/homeworkhelp/worldbook/
> atozgeography/n/387300.html

READ AND DISCOVER: Using library books, encyclopedias, or Internet sites, find the answer to these questions and record your answers in your Journal along with the source of your information (book, encyclopedia, website, etc).
1. When and why did the Separatists move to Holland? What did many of them do to earn a living while in Holland? Website suggestion:
> http://www.pilgrimhall.org/holland.htm

2. While in Holland, one of the Pilgrims ran a printing press to print religious books. Who owned and operated the printing press, and why were the books banned in England? Website suggestion:
> http://www.pilgrimhall.org/pilpress.htm

3. Why did they finally decide to leave Holland, and how did they go about it? Website suggestion:
> http://www.gospelcom.net/chi/GLIMPSEF/Glimpses/glmps020.shtml

RESOURCE: TO THE NEW WORLD
> http://kids.infoplease.lycos.com/ce6/history/A0860392.html

Thanksgiving
<u>WEEK ONE: Day Five</u>

This week, we've learned so much about Thanksgiving, and we will spend today reviewing some of the information that we've seen!

<u>Elementary Grades Windup</u>

Spend some time looking at and reviewing this week's pages in each student's Thanksgiving Journal.

1. Review the WOW'S (WORDS OF WISDOM) by writing them on 3x5 cards. Flip through the cards with the child to see how much they remember and review the meanings of the words. Save the cards for use throughout this unit study, having the student collect them in an envelope that they can decorate with their own drawings.

2. Talk about the four INTERESTING PEOPLE AND PLACES they have read about this week. Does the child remember some of the stories about these people and places? This is a great time to review what the student has written or narrated about some of these people in their Journal.

3. Have the student talk about their favorite part of this week's study. Was it a part of the READ AND DISCOVER questions, one of the INTERESTING PEOPLE AND PLACES, a favorite Internet site, or perhaps a favorite book?

4. Take some time today to work together on the family's Thanksgiving Album—gathering drawings, photos of project efforts, and souvenirs and putting them in the album.

<u>Junior/Senior High Windup</u>

Looking at your Thanksgiving Journal, review all of your work from this week with your parents.

1. Share your favorite findings of the week—your most interesting person, fact, or book. Why was it a favorite?

2. Have one of your parents review your WOW'S (WORDS OF WIDSOM) with you, asking you for the spelling and definitions of your words for this week.

3. Which Internet sites were the most interesting? Did you discover other sites that were also helpful?

4. This month provides the perfect opportunity for you to begin planning a service project for someone or a special family in your community! Take some time to think of someone that you would like to express your thanks to or share some of your blessings with. This week, write a plan for your service project, describing who it will be

for, what you need to do (step-by-step), and how to get the project completed. Try to plan to have it completed the week of Thanksgiving!

Additional Internet Sites

EASTONS BIBLE DICTIONARY—"DAVID"
   http://www.htmlbible.com/kjv30/easton/east0982.htm
COLORING PAGES FOR DAVID OF THE BIBLE
   http://www.coloring.ws/david.htm
REFORMATION IN ENGLAND
   http://elane.stanford.edu/wilson/Text/3d.html
MARTIN LUTHER'S LIFE
   http://mars.acnet.wnec.edu/%7Egrempel/courses/wc2/lectures/
   luther.html
MARTIN LUTHER
   http://www.bartleby.com/65/lu/Luther-M.html
KATIE LUTHER ESCAPES IN A FISH BARREL
   http://www.gospelcom.net/chi/GLIMPSEF/Glimpses/
   glmps076.shtml
NO POWER COULD SHUT MARTIN LUTHER UP
   http://www.gospelcom.net/chi/GLIMPSEF/Glimpses/
   glmps015.shtml
BRIEF HISTORY OF THE PILGRIMS
   http://school.discovery.com/homeworkhelp/worldbook/
   atozhistory/p/430295.html
PILGRIMS IN A STRANGE LAND
   http://www.gospelcom.net/chi/GLIMPSEF/Glimpses/
   glmps020.shtml
PRAYING HANDS BY A REFORMATION ARTIST
   http://www.gospelcom.net/chi/GLIMPSEF/Glimpses/
   glmps125.shtml
THE GENEVA BIBLE
   http://www.gospelcom.net/chi/HERITAGF/Issuenos/chl044.shtml
THE PILGRIMS
   http://school.discovery.com/homeworkhelp/worldbook/
   atozhistory/p/430295.html
TAKE A VIRTUAL TOUR OF LEIDEN, HOLLAND
   http://www.pilgrimhall.org/LeidenMuseum.htm

Thanksgiving

LEIDEN: CITY OF REFUGEES (PILGRIMS' LIVES IN LEIDEN)
http://www.leidenarchief.nl/pilgrims/html/pilgrims/top_html/history.html
EMIGRATION TO HOLLAND
http://kids.infoplease.lycos.com/ce6/history/A0860391.html
MAP OF THE UNITED KINGDOM AND EUROPE (SHOWS HOW FAR THE SEPARATISTS HAD TO TRAVEL WHEN THEY MOVED TO HOLLAND)
http://school.discovery.com/homeworkhelp/worldbook/atozpictures/mp000242.html
PILGRIMS — ARTICLE OF THE NATIONAL PARK SERVICE, CAPE COD
http://www.nps.gov/caco/heritage/pilgrims.html
MAP AND DESCRIPTION OF THE SEPARATISTS' FIRST ATTEMPT TO LEAVE ENGLAND FOR HOLLAND
http://www.rootsweb.com/~mosmd/1statt.htm
MAP AND DESCRIPTION OF THE SEPARATISTS' SECOND ATTEMPT TO LEAVE ENGLAND FOR HOLLAND
http://www.rootsweb.com/~mosmd/2ndatt.htm
EARLY COLONIAL HISTORY TIMELINE 1000–1700 A.D.
http://www.historyplace.com/unitedstates/revolution/rev-early.htm
RELIGION OF THE PILGRIMS
http://www.pilgrimhall.org/religion.htm
WILLIAM BREWSTER
http://members.aol.com/calebj/brewster.html
OVERFLOWING WITH THANKFULNESS
http://www.joyfulheart.com/holiday/overflowing.htm

Week One

<u>Some of Our Favorite Findings this Week</u>

It can be helpful to keep track of some of the favorite things you have discovered this week. Use this page to record some of these things for later review and further study.

Books: _____

_____

People: _____

_____

Places: _____

_____

Cool Words: _____

_____

Family Connections: _____

_____

Family Project of the Week: _____

_____

Internet Sites: _____

_____

_____

_____

Some Notes of Our Own: _____

_____

_____

_____

Thanksgiving
Week Two

This week will be used to focus on the Pilgrims' voyage to the New World.

Objectives

- Learn why the Separatists decided to leave Holland
- Find out how they obtained financial backing to make the trip and build a colony
- Discover how they traveled to America, what their journey was like, and what the ship, the *Mayflower*, was like
- Examine what some of the "Saints" and "Strangers" were like, what their roles were, and how they worked together

Thanksgiving

WEEK TWO: Day One

As we begin this week, we are going to take a look at the Separatists' decision to leave Holland and move to the New World and the work of Captain John Smith.

Elementary Grades

TODAY'S QUOTE: Copy today's quote into your Thanksgiving Journal: "Giving thanks always for all things unto God and the Father in the name of our Lord Jesus Christ."

—Ephesians 5:20

WOW: Look up the following words in the dictionary and write the words and their definitions in your Thanksgiving Journal:
1. water
2. cook
3. trip
4. enjoy

INTERESTING PEOPLE & PLACES: Using an encyclopedia or Internet site, look up **Captain John Smith.** Who was he, and why is he famous? Write or narrate a paragraph about Captain Smith for your Journal. Website suggestion:

http://www.jamestowne.org/history/johns.htm

READ AND DISCOVER: Using an encyclopedia, book, or Internet site, read the following questions and find the answers. Write your answers in your Journal.

1. Why did the Separatists decide to leave Holland (now called the Netherlands)? Find two reasons and describe them in your Journal. Website suggestion:

http://kids.infoplease.lycos.com/ce6/history/A0860391.html

2. In the APPENDIX of this book, you will find a story entitled, "Plymouth Colony," written by Mara Pratt in 1886. Read the first two sections of the story, stopping at the section, "Pilgrims in America." Can you see why the Separatists were unhappy and decided to go to America? Write a short story that describes what you think you would have felt if **YOU** were a Separatist, getting ready to leave Holland for the New World.

Week Two

Junior/Senior High

TODAY'S QUOTE: Copy today's quote into your Thanksgiving Journal: "Enter into his gates with thanksgiving, and into his courts with praise: be thankful unto him, and bless his name."

—Psalm 100:4

WOW: Look up the following words in the dictionary and write the words and their definitions in your Thanksgiving Journal:
1. adventure
2. agreement
3. pilgrimage
4. stranger

INTERESTING PEOPLE & PLACES: Using an encyclopedia or Internet site, look up **Captain John Smith.** Who was he, and how did his work help the passengers of the *Mayflower*? Summarize your answer in a paragraph in your Journal. Website suggestion:
   http://www.bartleby.com/225/0201.html

READ AND DISCOVER: Using library books, encyclopedias, or Internet sites, find the answer to these questions and record your answers in your Journal along with the source of your information (book, encyclopedia, website, etc).

1. Read the article about John Smith's work in the APPENDIX of this book, entitled, "Captain John Smith." What areas of New England did he survey and map, and who named it "New England"? What Indian was captured as a result of this expedition?

2. Read paragraphs 1–4 in the article, "The Plymouth Colony," by John A. Anderson (1894), which is included in the APPENDIX of this book. Describe the two different land grants made by King James, including the different geographical descriptions. What is meant by the word "parallel" as it is used in this article?

3. The main record that we have of the Separatists is the journal of William Bradford, *Of Plymouth Plantation.* He writes about their decision to leave Holland—summarize his comments in your own words and write them in your Journal. What is he talking about when he mentions the "beating of drums"? Website suggestion:
   http://www.pilgrimhall.org/bradjour.htm

WEEK TWO: Day Two

Now that the Pilgrims have decided to venture to the New World, we will learn more about their journey.

Elementary Grades

TODAY'S QUOTE: Copy today's quote into your Thanksgiving Journal: "Sixteen Twenty was the year, the *Mayflower* brought the Pilgrims here." —Genevieve Foster, in *Year of the Pilgrims 1620*

WOW: Look up the following words in the dictionary and write the words and their definitions in your Thanksgiving Journal:
1. boat
2. leak
3. help
4. obey

INTERESTING PEOPLE & PLACES: Using an encyclopedia or Internet site, look up **William Bradford.** Who was he, and why is he famous? Write or narrate a paragraph about William Bradford for your Journal. Website suggestion:

http://school.discovery.com/homeworkhelp/worldbook/
atozhistory/ b/073440.html

READ AND DISCOVER: Using an encyclopedia, book, or Internet site, read the following questions and find the answers. Write your answers in your Journal.

1. Who sailed on the *Mayflower*? Find the names of six passengers and list them in your Journal. Website suggestion:
http://www.plimoth.org/Library/maypass.htm

2. The Separatists had to find a way to pay for their trip to the New World and for their new colony. They made an agreement to work for a company for a certain number of years, sending back furs and other goods from America to England. How many years did they agree to do this work? Website suggestion:
http://kids.infoplease.lycos.com/ce6/history/A0860392.html

3. Where on the *Mayflower* did the passengers live? Were there any cannon, and where were they kept on the ship? Website suggestion (excellent diagram):
http://www.plimoth.org/Museum/Mayflower/mayflowe.htm

RESOURCE: MAKE GRAHAM CRACKER TURKEYS!
http://www.kidsdomain.com/craft/graham.html

Week Two

Junior/Senior High

TODAY'S QUOTE: Copy today's quote into your Thanksgiving Journal:
"Give thanks unto the LORD, call upon his name, make known his deeds among the people." —1 Chronicles 16:8

WOW: Look up the following words in the dictionary and write the words and their definitions in your Thanksgiving Journal:
1. journey
2. company
3. departure
4. Mayflower

INTERESTING PEOPLE & PLACES: Using an encyclopedia or Internet site, look up **William Bradford.** Who was he, and how did he become involved with the Separatists? What role did he play in the colony of Plymouth? Summarize your answer in two paragraphs in your Journal. Website:
    http://www.bartleby.com/65/br/Bradfd1590.html

READ AND DISCOVER: Using library books, encyclopedias, or Internet sites, find the answer to these questions and record your answers in your Journal along with the source of your information (book, encyclopedia, website, etc).

    1. Read paragraphs 5–6 in the article, "The Plymouth Colony" in the APPENDIX of this book and answer the following questions. What ship carried them from Holland to England? Once in England, how many ships did they use, initially, to sail to the New World? Why did they have to return to England?

    2. How many Pilgrims traveled to the New World on the *Mayflower*, and of these, how many were Leiden Separatists? What group became the leadership force of the Pilgrims and their colony? Website suggestions:
    http://www.pilgrimhall.org/mayfpass.htm
    http://kids.infoplease.lycos.com/ce6/history/A0832348.html

    3. How did the Pilgrims obtain financial backing for their new colony? What arrangements were made with businessmen in what country, and what were the terms of their venture? Websites:
    http://plimoth.org/Library/voyage.htm
    http://kids.infoplease.lycos.com/ce6/history/A0832348.html

Thanksgiving

WEEK TWO: Day Three

We will focus on some of the passengers of the *Mayflower* today, studying both the "Saints" and the "Strangers."

Elementary Grades

TODAY'S QUOTE: Copy today's quote into your Thanksgiving Journal: "There is something in every season, in every day, to celebrate with thanksgiving."

—Unknown

WOW: Look up the following words in the dictionary and write the words and their definitions in your Thanksgiving Journal:
1. travel
2. agree
3. ocean
4. land

INTERESTING PEOPLE & PLACES: Using an encyclopedia or Internet site, look up **John Carver.** Who was he, and why is he famous? Write or narrate a paragraph about John Carver for your Journal. Website suggestion:
http://school.discovery.com/homeworkhelp/worldbook/atozhistory/c/097840.html

READ AND DISCOVER: Using an encyclopedia, book, or Internet site, read the following questions and find the answers. Write your answers in your Thanksgiving Journal.

1. In the group of Pilgrims, some people were called "Saints" and some were called "Strangers." Who were they, and how were they different? Was John Carver a Saint or a Stranger? Website suggestion:
http://kids.infoplease.lycos.com/ce6/history/A0860392.html

2. The crew of the *Mayflower* was made up of interesting people, one of whom was John Alden. What was he hired to do on the *Mayflower*? Website suggestion:
http://www.plimoth.org/Library/mayflcre.htm

3. When did the Pilgrims leave England in the *Mayflower* (after they left the *Speedwell* because she kept leaking), and when did they arrive in America? How many days did their voyage take? Website suggestion:
http://www.plimoth.org/Library/Bibliography/bib-m1c.htm#mourt

Week Two

Junior/Senior High

TODAY'S QUOTE: Copy today's quote into your Thanksgiving Journal:
"Be careful for nothing; but in every thing by prayer and supplication with thanksgiving let your requests be made known unto God."
— Philippians 4:6

WOW: Look up the following words in the dictionary and write the words and their definitions in your Thanksgiving Journal:
1. nonconformist
2. passenger
3. reform
4. voyage

INTERESTING PEOPLE & PLACES: Using an encyclopedia or Internet site, look up **John Carver.** Who was he, and how was he involved with the Pilgrims? Summarize your answer in a paragraph in your Journal. Website suggestion: http://www.bartleby.com/65/ca/CarverJ.html

READ AND DISCOVER: Using books, encyclopedias, or websites, answer these questions and record your answers in your Journal with the source.

1. What was the difference between the "Saints" and the "Strangers"? With which group would these have been included: Miles Standish, John Alden, William Bradford, John Carver, and William Brewster? Out of 102 Pilgrims, how many were Saints and how many were Strangers? Website suggestion:
   http://kids.infoplease.lycos.com/ce6/history/A0860392.html

2. During the voyage, one of the crew members died, and William Bradford gives an interesting account of the crewman's death and circumstances in his book, *Of Plymouth Plantation.* Write this story in your own words in your Journal. Website suggestion:
   http://www.plimoth.org/Library/Bibliography/bib-m1c.htm#brad

3. What were the dates of the voyage from England to America, and from what town did they depart and where did they first set foot on land? How much time passed between their first departure from England with both the *Speedwell* and the *Mayflower* until their final departure in the *Mayflower* alone? How did this delay effect their opportunity to prepare for their first winter in America? Websites:
   http://www.pilgrimhall.org/bradfordJournalarrival.htm
   http://plimoth.org/Library/voyage.htm

Thanksgiving

WEEK TWO: Day Four

This day will be spent learning more about the *Mayflower*, some of the difficulties of the voyage, and how these difficulties were overcome.

Elementary Grades

TODAY'S QUOTE: Copy today's quote into your Thanksgiving Journal: "A ship in harbor is safe, but that is not what ships are built for."

—John A. Shedd

WOW: Look up the following words in the dictionary and write the words and their definitions in your Thanksgiving Journal:
1. colony
2. crowded
3. voyage
4. crew

INTERESTING PEOPLE & PLACES: Using an encyclopedia or Internet site, look up **Miles Standish.** Who was he, and how did he help the passengers of the *Mayflower*? Write or narrate a paragraph about Miles Standish for your Journal. Website suggestions:

http://kids.infoplease.lycos.com/ce6/people/A0846482.html
http://school.discovery.com/homeworkhelp/worldbook/
atozhistory/s/528980.html

READ AND DISCOVER: Using an encyclopedia, book, or Internet site, read the following questions and find the answers. Write your answers in your Journal.

1. What do we know about the *Mayflower*? How long was the ship? Draw a sketch of the *Mayflower* in your Journal. Website suggestions:

http://www.pilgrimhall.org/voymayfl.htm
http://members.aol.com/calcbj/mayflower_dimensions.html

2. What do you think the Pilgrims brought with them onboard the *Mayflower*? Remember that they didn't have much room on board the ship! They did bring along one large item that helped them save the ship in the midst of a storm—what was it? On the following website, there's a list of things that was given to newcomers in 1630. This might give you some ideas for your list:

http://www.pilgrimhall.org/provsns.htm

RESOURCE: GROW YOUR OWN CORN

http://www.kidsdomain.com/craft/grow.html

Week Two

Junior/Senior High

TODAY'S QUOTE: Copy today's quote into your Thanksgiving Journal:
"A little faith will bring your soul to heaven, but a lot of faith will bring heaven to your soul."
—Dwight L. Moody

WOW: Look up the following words in the dictionary and write the words and their definitions in your Thanksgiving Journal:

1. colony
2. charter
3. Virginia
4. daunting

INTERESTING PEOPLE & PLACES: Using an encyclopedia or Internet site, look up **Miles Standish.** Who was he, and what did he do to help the colony of Plymouth? Summarize your answer in a paragraph in your Journal. Website suggestion:

http://school.discovery.com/homeworkhelp/worldbook/
atozhistory/s/528980.html

READ AND DISCOVER: Using library books, encyclopedias, or Internet sites, find the answer to these questions and record your answers in your Journal along with the source of your information (book, encyclopedia, website, etc).

1. From William Bradford's journal, speaking of the Pilgrims as they stepped onto land in the New World: "What could not sustaine them but ye spirite of God & his grace? May not & ought not the children of these fathers rightly say: Our faithers were Englishmen which came over this great ocean, and were ready to perish in this willdernes; but they cried unto ye Lord, and he heard their voyce, and looked on their adversitie . . ." What do you think he meant when he wrote this, and was his idea about the future generations accurate? Website:

http://www.pilgrimhall.org/bradfordJournalarrival.htm

2. During the voyage, the Pilgrims experienced many difficulties. In your own words, describe some of the problems that they faced while traveling to America and how they overcame them. How many people were born, and how many died while en route? Website suggestion:

http://plimoth.org/Library/voyage.htm

Thanksgiving
WEEK TWO: Day Five

This week, we've learned so much about Thanksgiving, and we will spend today reviewing some of the information that we've learned!

Elementary Grades Windup

Spend some time looking at and reviewing this week's pages in each student's Thanksgiving Journal.

1. Review the WOW's (WORDS OF WISDOM) by writing them on 3x5 cards. Flip through the cards with the child to see how much they remember and review the meanings of the words. Save the cards for use throughout this unit study, having the student collect them in an envelope that they can decorate with their own drawings.

2. Talk about the four INTERESTING PEOPLE AND PLACES they have read about this week. Does the child remember some of the stories about these people and places? This is a great time to review what the student has written or narrated about some of these people in their Journal.

3. Have the student talk about their favorite part of this week's study. Was it a part of the READ AND DISCOVER questions, one of the INTERESTING PEOPLE AND PLACES, a favorite Internet site, or perhaps a favorite book?

4. Take some time today to work together on the family's Thanksgiving Album—gathering drawings, photos of project efforts, and souvenirs and putting them in the album.

Junior/Senior High Windup

Looking at your Thanksgiving Journal, review all of your work from this week with your parents.

1. Share your favorite findings of the week—your most interesting person, fact, or book. Why was it a favorite?

2. Have one of your parents review your WOW's (WORDS OF WIDSOM) with you, asking you for the spelling and definitions of your words for this week.

3. Which Internet sites were the most interesting? Did you discover other sites that were also helpful?

4. Only two weeks left now to complete your Thanksgiving service project! How is your project moving along—are you keeping up with the time schedule that you developed last week? Use today to make any adjustments, ask for help, and work on the project itself.

Additional Internet Sites

PILGRIM MEMORIALS AROUND THE WORLD
http://www.sail1620.org/m2k/history/monuments.htm

THE PILGRIMS' LIFE IN HOLLAND
http://plimoth.org/Library/holland.htm

TO THE NEW WORLD
http://kids.infoplease.lycos.com/ce6/history/A0860392.html

THE PILGRIMS DECIDE TO EMIGRATE, FROM WILLIAM BRADFORD'S JOURNAL
http://www.pilgrimhall.org/bradfordJournalemigrate.htm

WHAT IS A MAYFLOWER?
http://www.sail1620.org/m2k/history/whats.htm

PEREGRINE WHITE
http://school.discovery.com/homeworkhelp/worldbook/
atozhistory/w/601260.html

MAYFLOWER
http://school.discovery.com/homeworkhelp/worldbook/
atozhistory/m/350240.html

THE *MAYFLOWER II*
http://www.plimoth.org/Museum/Mayflower/mayflowe.htm

THE *MAYFLOWER*
http://kids.infoplease.lycos.com/ce6/history/A0832348.html

WILLIAM BREWSTER
http://school.discovery.com/homeworkhelp/worldbook/
atozhistory/b/076060.html

JOHN CARVER
http://www.encyclopedia.com/printablenew/02367.html

JOHN CARVER
http://kids.infoplease.lycos.com/ce6/people/A0810662.html

WILLIAM BRADFORD
http://www.encyclopedia.com/printablenew/01777.html

WILLIAM BRADFORD
http://school.discovery.com/homeworkhelp/worldbook/
atozhistory/b/073440.html

WILLIAM BRADFORD
http://kids.infoplease.lycos.com/ce6/people/A0808664.html

THE COURTSHIP OF MILES STANDISH
http://deil.lang.uiuc.edu/web.pages/Holidays/Standish.html
MILES STANDISH
http://kids.infoplease.lycos.com/ce6/people/A0846482.html
THE MAYFLOWER COMPACT
http://kids.infoplease.lycos.com/ce6/history/A0832350.html
PLYMOUTH: THE SETTLEMENT AND ITS HISTORY
http://pilgrims.net/plymouth/history/index.htm
CAPTAIN JOHN SMITH WRITES ABOUT THE PILGRIMS
http://members.aol.com/mayflo1620/smith.html
CAPTAIN JOHN SMITH'S MAP OF NEW ENGLAND
http://www.rootsweb.com/~mosmd/nemap.htm
DEPARTURE FOR NEW ENGLAND
http://plimoth.org/Library/depart.htm

<u>Some of Our Favorite Findings this Week</u>

It can be helpful to keep track of some of the favorite things you have discovered this week. Use this page to record some of these things for later review and further study.

Books: _____

_____

People: _____

_____

Places: _____

_____

Cool Words: _____

_____

Family Connections: _____

_____

Family Project of the Week: _____

_____

Internet Sites: _____

_____

_____

_____

Some Notes of Our Own: _____

_____

_____

_____

Thanksgiving
Week Three

This week will be used to focus on the Pilgrims' landing and their first winter.

Objectives

- Discover what the Pilgrims found when they reached America
- Explore the problems in finding a suitable location for their new colony
- Examine how the Pilgrims fared the first winter and some of their challenges
- Find out how the Pilgrims interacted with the Native Americans as they began to build their settlement

Thanksgiving

WEEK THREE: Day One

Last week we left the Pilgrims as they were arriving in the New World. Today, we will learn more about their landing and their search for a place to call home.

Elementary Grades

TODAY'S QUOTE: Copy today's quote into your Thanksgiving Journal: "Start by doing what's necessary, then do what's possible, and suddenly you are doing the impossible." —Saint Francis of Assisi

WOW: Look up the following words in the dictionary and write the words and their definitions in your Thanksgiving Journal:
1. settle
2. shoal
3. rules
4. explore

INTERESTING PEOPLE & PLACES: Using a map, encyclopedia, or Internet site, find **Massachusetts.** Draw a map of Massachusetts in your Journal. Make sure to mark the towns of Plymouth and Cape Cod. Website:
http://www.lib.utexas.edu/maps/united_states/massachusetts_90.jpg

READ AND DISCOVER: Using an encyclopedia, book, or Internet site, read the following questions and find the answers. Write or narrate your answers for your Journal.

1. Imagine that you have been traveling, in a sailing ship that is crowded and dreary—for two months! What would you have thought when you finally saw **LAND** from the deck of the ship? Imagine that you are one of the first Pilgrim children to set foot in the New World, and write a story that describes what you did when you finally landed!

2. What is the name of the agreement that the Pilgrims wrote and signed before beginning to build the new colony. Why do you think that it was important—remember the Saints and the Strangers? Could this help them get along? Website suggestion: http://school. discovery.com/homeworkhelp/worldbook/atozhistory/m/350260.html http://plimoth.org/Library/compact.htm

RESOURCES: HANDS AND FEET TURKEY
http://kidsdomain.com/craft/hand-tur.html

Week Three

Junior/Senior High

TODAY'S QUOTE: Copy today's quote into your Thanksgiving Journal: "Let us come before his presence with thanksgiving, and make a joyful noise unto him with psalms." —Psalm 95:2

WOW: Look up the following words in the dictionary and write the words and their definitions in your Thanksgiving Journal:
1. exploration
2. suitable
3. settlement
4. valid

INTERESTING PEOPLE & PLACES: Using an encyclopedia or Internet site, look up **Massachusetts.** Draw a map of Massachusetts in your Journal, and label Cape Cod, Plymouth, and Provincetown on your map. Website:
http://school.discovery.com/homeworkhelp/worldbook/
atozpictures/lr000991.html

READ AND DISCOVER: Using library books, encyclopedias, or Internet sites, find the answer to these questions and record your answers in your Journal along with the source of your information (book, encyclopedia, website, etc).

1. What were the Pilgrims like as people? Choose one of the passengers and write a short story about that person (it can be fact or fiction). Develop your story so that it explains why they traveled to America, what their family was like, and any other details that you want to include in your story.

2. Another primary source that describes the Pilgrims' days in early Plymouth is called *Mourt's Relation* and is believed to have been written by Edward Winslow and William Bradford. The authors describe their journey across the ocean and their first impressions of the New World. After reading their report of arrival in the bay of Cape Cod, write a description of the timber and animal life that they mention in this passage. How many kinds of trees are listed by name? Here is a website suggestion:
http://www.plimoth.org/Library/Bibliography/bib-m1c.htm#mourt

RESOURCES: PAINTED PILGRIMS, AN ART STUDY FOR GRADES 6–12
http://www.pilgrimhall.org/EdnPaintedPilgims.htm

Thanksgiving

WEEK THREE: Day Two

This day will be spent learning more about the Pilgrims' search for a place to settle and the early days at Plymouth.

Elementary Grades

TODAY'S QUOTE: Copy today's quote into your Thanksgiving Journal:
"Keep your fears to yourself, but share your courage with others."
–Robert Louis Stevenson

WOW: Look up the following words in the dictionary and write the words and their definitions in your Thanksgiving Journal:
1. chores
2. eat
3. gun
4. search

INTERESTING PEOPLE & PLACES: Using an encyclopedia or Internet site, look up **Priscilla Mullins.** Did she travel over on the *Mayflower*, and who did she marry? Website suggestion:
http://school.discovery.com/homeworkhelp/worldbook/
atozhistory/a/011810.html

READ AND DISCOVER: Using an encyclopedia, book, or Internet site, read the following questions and find the answers. Write or narrate the answers for your Journal.
1. Read the rest of the story, "Plymouth Colony," by Mara Pratt in the APPENDIX of this book, beginning with "The Pilgrims in America." What was the name of the baby boy that the author describes, and what does his name mean?
2. Why did the Pilgrims choose to go on to Plymouth after first landing by Provincetown? Website suggestion:
http://school.discovery.com/homeworkhelp/worldbook/
atozhistory/p/435620.html
(read the section on The Founding of Plymouth Colony)

RESOURCE:
APPLE PRINTING CRAFT
http://www.kidsdomain.com/craft/appleprint.html

Week Three

Junior/Senior High

TODAY'S QUOTE: Copy today's quote into your Thanksgiving Journal:
"To believe in the things you see and touch is no belief at all; but to believe in the unseen is a triumph and a blessing."

—Abraham Lincoln

WOW: Look up the following words in the dictionary and write the words and their definitions in your Thanksgiving Journal:
1. sickness
2. determination
3. hardship
4. colonial

INTERESTING PEOPLE & PLACES: Using an encyclopedia or Internet site, look up **Priscilla Mullins.** Did she travel over on the *Mayflower*, and who did she marry? A famous poem was written about this marriage by one of their descendents—what is the name of the poem, and who wrote it? Website suggestions:

http://school.discovery.com/homeworkhelp/worldbook/
atozhistory/a/011810.html

http://members.aol.com/calebj/passenger.html

READ AND DISCOVER: Using library books, encyclopedias, or Internet sites, find the answer to these questions and record your answers in your Journal along with the source of your information (book, encyclopedia, website, etc).

1. Read paragraphs 7–8 in the article, "The Plymouth Colony" in the APPENDIX of this book. To add to this description, read about their landing and exploration in William Bradford's journal, *Of Plymouth Plantation.* Summarize their efforts in your Journal, describing their findings, confrontations, and final choice of settlement. Website suggestions: http://www.stormfax.com/thanksgv.htm

http://members.aol.com/calebj/bradford_Journal9.html

http://www.pilgrimhall.org/bradfordJournalclarks.htm

2. What did the Pilgrims write and sign before building Plymouth Colony? Why was this important, and what might have happened if they had not reached an agreement? Website suggestions:

http://www.pilgrimhall.org/compcon.htm

http://www.gospelcom.net/chi/DAILYF/2000/11/
daily-11-21-2000.shtml

Thanksgiving

WEEK THREE: Day Three

This day will be spent learning about the many trials of the first winter, and how the Pilgrims managed to survive.

Elementary Grades

TODAY'S QUOTE: Copy today's quote into your Thanksgiving Journal:
"Fear knocked at the door. Faith answered. And lo, no one was there."
—Unknown

WOW: Look up the following words in the dictionary and write the words and their definitions in your Thanksgiving Journal:
1. attack
2. protect
3. hunt
4. work

INTERESTING PEOPLE & PLACES: Using an encyclopedia or Internet site, look up find a description of the **Wampanoag Indians.** Write or narrate a paragraph about them for your Journal. Website suggestion:
http://kids.infoplease.lycos.com/ce6/society/A0851417.html

READ AND DISCOVER: Using an encyclopedia, book, or Internet site, read the following questions and find the answers. Write or narrate your answers for your Journal.
1. The Pilgrims' first winter in Plymouth was a very difficult one. What kinds of problems did they face? Website suggestions:
http://kids.infoplease.lycos.com/ce6/history/A0860438.html
http://school.discovery.com/homeworkhelp/worldbook/
   atozhistory/p/435620.html
2. Through all of their problems, the Pilgrims stayed strong in their faith that God was with them. When times are the hardest, it can be hard to keep your faith in God—but that is the time to keep it the strongest! Was there ever a time that bad things happened and tested your faith? Describe this time or how you might feel if something bad happened to you. Keep your faith!

RESOURCE:
FALL WREATH
   http://www.kidsdomain.com/craft/autumnwreath.html

Week Three

<u>Junior/Senior High</u>

TODAY'S QUOTE: Copy today's quote into your Thanksgiving Journal:
"The wise person in the storm prays God, not for safety from danger, but for deliverance from fear. It is the storm within which endangers us, not the storm without."

—Ralph Waldo Emerson

WOW: Look up the following words in the dictionary and write the words and their definitions in your Thanksgiving Journal:
1. construction
2. burial
3. starvation
4. defense

INTERESTING PEOPLE & PLACES: Using an encyclopedia or Internet site, look up **Wamponoag Indians.** Who were they, and how did they interact with the Pilgrims? Summarize your answer in a paragraph in your Journal. Website suggestions:
> http://www.plimoth.org/Library/Wampanoag/wamp.htm
> http://www.plimoth.org/Museum/Hobbamock/hobbamoc.htm

READ AND DISCOVER: Using library books, encyclopedias, or Internet sites, find the answer to these questions and record your answers in your Journal along with the source of your information (book, encyclopedia, website, etc).

1. Read paragraph 9 in the article, "The Plymouth Colony" in the APPENDIX of this book. To add to this description, read the section in William Bradford's journal that describes, "In these hard & difficulte beginings. . ." Write a description of their first winter in your own words, and include the names of the two Pilgrims that Bradford commends for taking care of the sick during their difficult beginnings. Website suggestions:
> http://www.pilgrimhall.org/bradfordJournalstarving.htm
> http://www.plimoth.org/Library/firstw.htm

2. How many Pilgrims survived the winter? They could have given up and sailed back to England with the *Mayflower*—did any sail back? What do you think gave them strength? Website suggestions:
> http://www.family.org/fofmag/sh/a0013711.html
> http://plimoth.org/Education/piltriv.htm

Thanksgiving

WEEK THREE: Day Four

Today we will learn more about the Native Americans that were involved with the Pilgrims and how they all worked together to keep the peace.

Elementary Grades

TODAY'S QUOTE: Copy today's quote into your Thanksgiving Journal:
"Faith is like radar that sees through the fog."
—Corrie Ten Boom

WOW: Look up the following words in the dictionary and write the words and their definitions in your Thanksgiving Journal:
1. bow
2. arrow
3. teach
4. survive

INTERESTING PEOPLE & PLACES: Using an encyclopedia or Internet site, look up **Squanto.** Why is he famous, and how did he help the Pilgrims? Write a paragraph about him for your Journal. Website suggestion:
   http://school.discovery.com/homeworkhelp/worldbook/
      atozhistory/s/527280.html

READ AND DISCOVER: Using an encyclopedia, book, or Internet site, read the following questions and find the answers. Write or narrate your answers for your Journal.
   1. Who was Samoset? How did he help the Pilgrims? Write or narrate a paragraph about Samoset for your Journal. Websites:
   http://pilgrims.net/native_americans/samoset.html
   http://school.discovery.com/homeworkhelp/worldbook/
      atozhistory/s/487620.html
   2. What did the Pilgrims' clothing look like? Draw a picture of a Pilgrim man, woman, or child in the kinds of clothing that they wore. Website suggestions: http://plimoth.org/Library/mens.htm
   http://plimoth.org/Library/womens.htm
   3. What did the Indians' clothing look like? Draw a picture of an Indian man or woman in the kinds of clothing that they wore. Here is a website suggestion:
   http://plimoth.org/Library/Wampanoag/nacostum.htm

Week Three

Junior/Senior High

TODAY'S QUOTE: Copy today's quote into your Thanksgiving Journal: "The Pilgrims made seven times more graves than huts. No Americans have been more impoverished than these who, nevertheless, set aside a day of thanksgiving."   —H.U. Westermayer

WOW: Look up the following words in the dictionary and write the words and their definitions in your Thanksgiving Journal:
1. meetinghouse
2. government
3. governor
4. courageous

INTERESTING PEOPLE & PLACES: Using an encyclopedia or Internet site, look up **Squanto.** Who was he, and how did he help the settlers of Plymouth? What was his real name, and how did he learn to speak English? Summarize your answer in a paragraph in your Journal. Website suggestions:

http://members.aol.com/calebj/squanto.html
http://school.discovery.com/homeworkhelp/worldbook/
    atozhistory/s/527280.html

READ AND DISCOVER: Using library books, encyclopedias, or Internet sites, find the answer to these questions and record your answers in your Journal along with the source of your information (book, encyclopedia, website, etc).

1. Who was Samoset? How did he come to know the colonists of Plymouth, and how did he help them? Summarize your answer in a paragraph in your Journal. Website suggestions:

http://pilgrims.net/native_americans/samoset.html
http://school.discovery.com/homeworkhelp/worldbook/
    atozhistory/s/487620.html

2. What was the difference in the clothing worn by the Pilgrims and the Indians? What were their clothes made of? Draw sketches of a man and woman of both Pilgrims and Indians in the clothing that your research indicates they might have worn. Website suggestions:

http://plimoth.org/Library/mens.htm
http://plimoth.org/Library/womens.htm
http://plimoth.org/Library/Wampanoag/nacostum.htm

Thanksgiving

WEEK THREE: Day Five

This week, we've learned so much about Thanksgiving, and we will spend today reviewing some of the information that we've found!

Elementary Grades Windup

Spend some time looking at and reviewing this week's pages in each student's Thanksgiving Journal.

1. Review the WOW's (WORDS OF WISDOM) by writing them on 3x5 cards. Flip through the cards with the child to see how much they remember and review the meanings of the words. Save the cards for use throughout this unit study, having the student collect them in an envelope that they can decorate with their own drawings.

2. Talk about the four INTERESTING PEOPLE AND PLACES they have read about this week. Does the child remember some of the stories about these people and places? This is a great time to review what the student has written or narrated about some of these people in their Journal.

3. Have the student talk about their favorite part of this week's study. Was it a part of the READ AND DISCOVER questions, one of the INTERESTING PEOPLE AND PLACES, a favorite Internet site, or perhaps a favorite book?

4. Take some time today to work together on the family's Thanksgiving Album—gathering drawings, photos of project efforts, and souvenirs and putting them in the album.

Junior/Senior High Windup

Looking at your Thanksgiving Journal, review all of your work from this week with your parents.

1. Share your favorite findings of the week—your most interesting person, fact, or book. Why was it a favorite?

2. Have one of your parents review your WOW's (WORDS OF WIDSOM) with you, asking you for the spelling and definitions of your words for this week.

3. Which Internet sites were the most interesting? Did you discover other sites that were also helpful?

4. One week left to finish your Thanksgiving service project! Use today to work on it, checking your progress against your plan and asking for assistance if you need it. Are there any other supplies that you need? Plan your work and work your plan—your efforts are going to bless someone special!

Week Three

Additional Internet Sites

A VIRTUAL TOUR OF PLYMOUTH PLANTATION
http://www.plimoth.org/Virtualtour/welcome.htm

THE LANDING OF THE PILGRIMS (INTERESTING PRINT)
http://www.americaslibrary.gov/pages/jb_1492-1763_subj_e.html

MAYFLOWER II
http://www.plymouthguide.com/mayflower.html

THE FOUNDING OF PLYMOUTH COLONY
http://kids.infoplease.lycos.com/ce6/history/A0860437.html

THANKSGIVING: THE WHOLE STORY (FOCUS ON THE FAMILY)
http://www.family.org/fofmag/sh/a0013711.html

MAYFLOWER COMPACT
http://school.discovery.com/homeworkhelp/worldbook/
atozhistory/m/350260.html

MAYFLOWER COMPACT
http://kids.infoplease.lycos.com/ce6/history/A0832350.html

THE MAYFLOWER COMPACT
http://www.law.ou.edu/hist/mayflow.html

THE WAMPANOAG PEOPLE
http://www.plimoth.org/Library/Wampanoag/wamp.htm

THE NATIVE AMERICANS
http://members.aol.com/calebj/indians.html

EARLY DAYS IN PLYMOUTH COLONY (INDIANS' INTERACTION)
http://www.pilgrimhall.org/arrival.htm

MASSASOIT
http://www.plimoth.org/Library/massasoi.htm

HISTORY OF SQUANTO
http://members.aol.com/calebj/squanto.html

JOHN AND PRISCILLA ALDEN
http://school.discovery.com/homeworkhelp/worldbook/
atozhistory/a/011810.html

MOURT'S RELATION
http://members.aol.com/calebj/mourt.html

BRIEF HISTORY OF PLYMOUTH COLONY
http://school.discovery.com/homeworkhelp/worldbook/
atozhistory/p/435620.html

Thanksgiving

AMERICAN HISTORY TIMELINE: 1600–1625
   http://americanhistory.about.com/library/timelines/
      bltimeline1600.htm
THE NEW ENGLAND COLONIES
   http://www.americancolonialhistory.com/article1005.html?printable=y
THEIR FIRST WINTER
   http://www.plimoth.org/Library/firstw.htm
PILGRIM CLOTHING
   http://www.plimoth.org/Library/costume.htm
PILGRIMS' PROVISIONS LIST
   http://www.plimoth.org/Library/massprov.htm
WAMPANOAG CLOTHING FOR THE 17TH CENTURY
   http://www.plimoth.org/Library/Wampanoag/nacostum.htm
17TH CENTURY WOMEN'S AND CHILDREN'S CLOTHING
   http://www.plimoth.org/Library/womens.htm
17TH CENTURY MEN'S CLOTHING
   http://www.plimoth.org/Library/mens.htm
ARM & ARMOR OF THE PILGRIMS
   http://www.pilgrimhall.org/ArmsIntro.htm
THE EXPLORING PARTY
   http://www.pilgrimhall.org/bradfordJournalclarks.htm
THE WINTER WEATHER OF 1620–1621
   http://www.stormfax.com/thanksgv.htm
THE LANDING OF THE PILGRIMS
   http://www.pilgrimhall.org/arrival.htm
RELIC OF THE *MAYFLOWER*—ANNOTATIONS UPON THE BOOK OF PSALMS, 1617
(remember all of the psalms that mention praise and thanksgiving?)
   http://www.lva.lib.va.us/sb/exhibits/treasures/rare/rar-k2.htm
INTERESTING FACTS ABOUT THE PILGRIMS, THE WAMPANOAG, & PLYMOUTH
   http://plimoth.org/Library/interest.htm
PILGRIM TRIVIA
   http://plimoth.org/Education/piltriv.htm
WALKING THE PILGRIM PATH
   http://www.plymouthguide.com/pilgwalk.html

<u>Some of Our Favorite Findings this Week</u>

It can be helpful to keep track of some of the favorite things you have discovered this week. Use this page to record some of these things for later review and further study.

Books: _____

_____

People: _____

_____

Places: _____

_____

Cool Words: _____

_____

Family Connections: _____

_____

Family Project of the Week: _____

_____

Internet Sites: _____

_____

_____

_____

Some Notes of Our Own: _____

_____

_____

_____

Thanksgiving
Week Four

This week will be used to focus on the Pilgrims' first crops and their harvest celebration.

Objectives

- Discover the crops the Pilgrims planted that first spring
- Explore the early development of Plymouth settlement
- Find out more about the harvest celebration—what the festival was like, who attended, and what they ate
- Learn more about the Wampanoag Indians—what they planted and how they lived
- Study the history of the Thanksgiving holiday in America

Thanksgiving
WEEK FOUR: Day One

Today we will find out more about the Pilgrims' spring planting and the development of their colony.

Elementary Grades

TODAY'S QUOTE: Copy today's quote into your Thanksgiving Journal:
"For each new morning with its light,
For rest and shelter of the night,
For health and food, for love and friends,
For everything Thy goodness sends."
—Ralph Waldo Emerson

WOW: Look up the following words in the dictionary and write the words and their definitions in your Thanksgiving Journal:
1. corn
2. fish
3. pumpkin
4. deer

INTERESTING PEOPLE & PLACES: Using an encyclopedia or Internet site, look up **George Washington**. Who was he, and why do we remember him? Write or narrate a paragraph about George Washington for your Thanksgiving Journal.

READ AND DISCOVER: Using an encyclopedia, book, or Internet site, read the following questions and find the answers. Write or narrate your answers for your Journal.
1. In 1789, our first president set aside a special day to give thanks to God! What day did he set aside for this day of thanksgiving? Website suggestion: http://www.night.net/thanksgiving/kwash-11.html
2. What did the Pilgrims plant that first spring in Plymouth? Website suggestion: http://www.pilgrimhall.org/1stthnks.htm
3. Draw a sketch of the early Plymouth settlement or a sketch of what one of their homes might have looked like. Website suggestion:
http://www.plimoth.org/Museum/Pilgrim_Village/1627.htm
(excellent clickable diagram that links to photos of each rebuilt house)

RESOURCE: THANKSGIVING COLORING AND ACTIVITY PAGES
http://www.sail1620.org/m2k/kids/colorbook/default.html

Week Four

Junior/Senior High

TODAY'S QUOTE: Copy today's quote into your Thanksgiving Journal: "God gave you a gift of 86,400 seconds today. Have you used one to say thank you?"

—William A. Ward

WOW: Look up the following words in the dictionary and write the words and their definitions in your Thanksgiving Journal:
1. shortage
2. provisions
3. scripture
4. agriculture

INTERESTING PEOPLE & PLACES: Using an encyclopedia or Internet site, look up **George Washington.** What role did he play in American history? Summarize your answer in a paragraph in your Journal.

READ AND DISCOVER: Using library books, encyclopedias, or Internet sites, find the answer to these questions and record your answers in your Journal along with the source of your information (book, encyclopedia, website, etc).

1. Read George Washington's Thanksgiving Proclamation of 1789, and compare it to a more recent presidential Thanksgiving proclamation. How do they differ, and how are they alike? Website suggestions:

http://www.whitehouse.gov
http://www.gtbe.org/documents/presidential_thanksgiving.html
http://www.virginia.edu/gwpapers/thanksgiving/transcript.html

2. What did the Pilgrims plant that first spring in Plymouth? What did the Native Americans of New England plant? Website suggestions:

http://www.pilgrimhall.org/1stthnks.htm
http://www.plimoth.org/Library/Wampanoag/wamphort.htm
http://www.plimoth.org/Library/Wampanoag/nacrops.htm

3. Draw a diagram of the Plymouth Settlement, and a sketch of one of the homes. Website suggestion:

http://www.plimoth.org/Museum/Pilgrim_Village/1627.htm
(excellent clickable diagram that links to photos of each rebuilt house)

Thanksgiving

WEEK FOUR: Day Two

Today we investigate that first harvest celebration, learning more about the festivities and the people that participated in the feast.

Elementary Grades

TODAY'S QUOTE: Copy today's quote into your Thanksgiving Journal:
"Land of the pilgrims' pride:
From every mountainside,
Let freedom ring."
—from the song *America*, by Samuel Smith

WOW: Look up the following words in the dictionary and write the words and their definitions in your Thanksgiving Journal:
1. turkey
2. kernel
3. gather
4. harvest

INTERESTING PEOPLE & PLACES: Using an encyclopedia or Internet site, look up **Abraham Lincoln.** Who was he? Write or narrate a paragraph about Abraham Lincoln for your Journal.

READ AND DISCOVER: Using an encyclopedia, book, or Internet site, read the following questions and find the answers. Write or narrate your answers for your Journal.
1. Who proclaimed the Pilgrim's day of celebration in the autumn of 1621, and what were they celebrating? Website suggestion:
http://www.pilgrimhall.org/1stthnks.htm#Bradford
2. Who attended this big celebration? What kinds of food did they eat? Website suggestions:
http://members.aol.com/calebj/thanksgiving.html
http://www.plimoth.org/Library/Thanksgiving/1stbill.htm
3. In 1863, what did Abraham Lincoln do that began our annual Thanksgiving holiday celebrations? Website suggestion:
http://plimoth.org/Library/Thanksgiving/thanks63.htm

RESOURCE:
THANKSGIVING WORD SEARCH PUZZLE
http://www.sail1620.org/m2k/kids/puzzle.htm

Week Four

<u>Junior/Senior High</u>

TODAY'S QUOTE: Copy today's quote into your Thanksgiving Journal:
"Our harvest being gotten in, our governor sent four men on fowling, that so we might after a special manner rejoice together after we had gathered the fruit of our labors."

—Edward Winslow, *Mourt's Relation* (1621)

WOW: Look up the following words in the dictionary and write the words and their definitions in your Thanksgiving Journal:
1. hopeful   3. forefather
2. gratitude   4. celebration

INTERESTING PEOPLE & PLACES: Using an encyclopedia or Internet site, look up **Abraham Lincoln.** Write or narrate a paragraph that describes him and how he is connected with the Thanksgiving holiday that we celebrate every year. Website suggestion:
http://plimoth.org/Library/Thanksgiving/thanks63.htm

READ AND DISCOVER: Using library books, encyclopedias, or Internet sites, find the answer to these questions and record your answers in your Journal along with the source of your information (book, encyclopedia, website, etc).

1. Read both accounts of the harvest festival—the one written by William Bradford in *Of Plymouth Plantation* and the one by Edward Winslow in *Mourt's Relation*. Write your own description of this celebration. Website suggestions:
http://www.pilgrimhall.org/1stthnks.htm#Bradford
http://plimoth.org/Library/Thanksgiving/thnksref.htm

2. What types of food did they eat at the celebration? How many married Pilgrim women were still alive to prepare this feast, and how many people attended? Website suggestions:
http://www.pilgrimhall.org/1stthnks.htm
http://members.aol.com/calebj/thanksgiving.html

3. The Separatists came to this country to have the freedom to worship in their own way. Find the amendment to the Constitution that guarantees this right that they helped to establish, and copy it into your Journal. Website suggestion:
http://school.discovery.com/homeworkhelp/worldbook/
atozhistory/c/131000.html

Thanksgiving

WEEK FOUR: Day Three

Today we will learn more about the Native Americans and the coming of new settlers to Plymouth.

Elementary Grades

TODAY'S QUOTE: Copy today's quote into your Thanksgiving Journal:
"The LORD hath done great things for us; whereof we are glad."
—Psalm 126:3

WOW: Look up the following words in the dictionary and write the words and their definitions in your Thanksgiving Journal:
1. peace
2. Indian
3. treaty
4. family

INTERESTING PEOPLE & PLACES: Using an encyclopedia or Internet site, look up **Massasoit**. Who was he? Write or narrate a paragraph about Massasoit for your Journal. Website suggestions:
http://pilgrims.net/native_americans/massasoit.html
http://school.discovery.com/homeworkhelp/worldbook/
atozhistory/m/348340.html

READ AND DISCOVER: Using an encyclopedia, book, or Internet site, read the following questions and find the answers. Write or narrate your answers for your Journal.

1. After the *Mayflower* brought over the very first Pilgrims, many other Separatists followed. Wanting the newcomers to bring the right supplies, Edward Winslow sent advice for the new settlers to Plymouth in 1622. What would **YOU** have recommended that they bring? What kind of fruit juice did he recommend that they bring? Website suggestion: http://www.pilgrimhall.org/provsnswinslow.htm

2. What did the Wampanoag Indians' homes look like? Draw one in your Journal or build one out of modeling clay. Website suggestion: http://www.plimoth.org/Museum/Hobbamock/hobbamoc.htm

3. What kinds of vegetables did the Wampanoag grow? Website suggestion: http://www.plimoth.org/Library/Wampanoag/nacrops.htm

RESOURCES: 17TH CENTURY RIDDLES
http://www.plimoth.org/Education/riddles.htm

Week Four

Junior/Senior High

TODAY'S QUOTE: Copy today's quote into your Thanksgiving Journal:
"Belief is a truth held in the mind; faith is a fire in the heart."
— Joseph Fort Newton

WOW: Look up the following words in the dictionary and write the words and their definitions in your Thanksgiving Journal:
1. peaceful
2. friendly
3. venison
4. sachem

INTERESTING PEOPLE & PLACES: Using an encyclopedia or Internet site, look up **Massasoit**. What interaction did he have with the early colonists of Plymouth? Summarize your answer in a paragraph in your Journal. Website suggestions:

http://pilgrims.net/native_americans/massasoit.html
http://school.discovery.com/homeworkhelp/worldbook/
   atozhistory/m/348340.html

READ AND DISCOVER: Using library books, encyclopedias, or Internet sites, find the answer to these questions and record your answers in your Journal along with the source of your information (book, encyclopedia, website, etc).

1. Of all of the attendees at the "First Thanksgiving," how many were Pilgrims and how many were Native Americans? How many Pilgrim men were there, and how many young children? Website suggestions: http://www.pilgrimhall.org/1stthnks.htm
http://plimoth.org/Education/piltriv.htm

2. Edward Winslow wrote a few recommendations to advise new settlers what to bring with them when leaving England for Plymouth in 1622. Make a list of his suggestions in your own words. What do **YOU** think were the three most important things that they should bring? Website suggestion:

http://www.pilgrimhall.org/provsnswinslow.htm

RESOURCES: LETTER TO FAMILY AND FRIENDS FROM WILLIAM HILTON OF PLYMOUTH (arrived in Plymouth in 1621 on the good ship *Fortune*)
http://members.aol.com/calebj/hilton.html

59

Thanksgiving

WEEK FOUR: Day Four

This day will be spent learning more of the history of the American Thanksgiving holiday.

Elementary Grades

TODAY'S QUOTE: Copy today's quote into your Thanksgiving Journal:
"For thou shalt eat the labour of thine hands: happy shalt thou be, and it shall be well with thee."

— Psalm 128:2

WOW: Look up the following words in the dictionary and write the words and their definitions in your Thanksgiving Journal:
1. thankful
2. succeed
3. crops
4. share

INTERESTING PEOPLE & PLACES: Using an encyclopedia or Internet site, look up **Edward Winslow.** Write or narrate a paragraph about him for your Journal. Website suggestion:
> http://school.discovery.com/homeworkhelp/worldbook/
> atozhistory/w/606740.html

READ AND DISCOVER: Using an encyclopedia, book, or Internet site, read the following questions and find the answers. Write or narrate your answers for your Journal.

1. The first national day of Thanksgiving was proclaimed by the Continental Congress on November 1, 1777. Who did Congress say that we should thank for America's blessings? Website suggestion:
> http://plimoth.org/Library/Thanksgiving/1777.htm

2. Americans have celebrated Thanksgiving every year since the proclamation in 1863. What is the date of Thanksgiving this year? Thanksgiving is now observed on the fourth Thursday of November, and this was signed into law by President Franklin Roosevelt. When did this happen? Website suggestion:
> http://plimoth.org/Library/Thanksgiving/th2.htm

3. Write or narrate a short story that describes your favorite Thanksgiving, describing what made it the best one yet! Who was there, and what did you do on that day?

Week Four

Junior/Senior High

TODAY'S QUOTE: Copy today's quote into your Thanksgiving Journal:
"The private and personal blessings we enjoy—the blessings of immunity, safeguard, liberty, and integrity—deserve the thanksgiving of a whole life." —Jeremy Taylor

WOW: Look up the following words in the dictionary and write the words and their definitions in your Thanksgiving Journal:
1. festivities
2. successful
3. contribute
4. faithful

INTERESTING PEOPLE & PLACES: Using an encyclopedia or Internet site, look up **Edward Winslow.** Write a descriptive biography about him in two paragraphs in your Journal. Website suggestion:
http://school.discovery.com/homeworkhelp/worldbook/
atozhistory/w/606740.html

READ AND DISCOVER: Using library books, encyclopedias, or Internet sites, find the answer to these questions and record your answers in your Journal along with the source of your information.

1. The first national day of Thanksgiving was proclaimed by the Continental Congress on November 1, 1777—on the occasion of what event? Find a copy of this proclamation, and copy the first sentence in your Journal, noticing exactly who is credited with providing their blessings and bounties. Website suggestion:
http://plimoth.org/Library/Thanksgiving/1777.htm

2. Write a one-page description of three blessings that you are **MOST** thankful for, and why you are thankful for them. Write the story as if you were trying to explain these blessings to someone your own age from a foreign country.

3. What president signed a bill that established Thanksgiving as the fourth Thursday in November? When do we celebrate Thanksgiving this year? Website suggestion:
http://plimoth.org/Library/Thanksgiving/th2.htm

4. What is celebrated on Forefathers' Day, and when and where is it celebrated? Website suggestion:
http://plimoth.org/Library/forefath.htm

WEEK FOUR: Day Five

Throughout this study, we've learned so much about Thanksgiving, and we will spend today reviewing some of the information that we've learned!

Elementary Grades Windup

Spend some time looking at and reviewing this week's pages in each student's Thanksgiving Journal.

1. Review the WOW's (WORDS OF WISDOM) by writing them on 3x5 cards. Flip through the cards with the child to see how much they remember and review the meanings of the words. Save the cards for review use later, having the student collect them in an envelope that they can decorate with their own drawings.

2. Talk about the four INTERESTING PEOPLE AND PLACES they have read about this week. Does the child remember some of the stories about these people and places? This is a great time to review what the student has written or narrated about some of these people in their Journal.

3. Have the student talk about their favorite part of this week's study. Was it a part of the READ AND DISCOVER questions, one of the INTERESTING PEOPLE AND PLACES, a favorite Internet site, or perhaps a favorite book?

4. Take some time today to work together on the family's Thanksgiving Album—gathering drawings, photos of project efforts, and souvenirs and putting them in the album.

Junior/Senior High Windup

Looking at your Thanksgiving Journal, review all of your work from this week with your parents.

1. Share your favorite findings of the week—your most interesting person, fact, or book. Why was it a favorite?

2. Have one of your parents review your WOW's (WORDS OF WIDSOM) with you, asking you for the spelling and definitions of your words for this week.

3. Which Internet sites were the most interesting? Did you discover other sites that were also helpful?

4. Wrap up your service project today, and present the final product! I hope you have blessed others with your efforts and that you continue to share your blessings from now on. Happy Thanksgiving, and may God bless you abundantly!

Week Four
Additional Internet Sites

THANKSGIVING HYMNS TO ENJOY TOGETHER

WE GATHER TOGETHER
http://www.cyberhymnal.org/htm/w/e/wegattog.htm
COME, YE THANKFUL PEOPLE, COME
http://www.cyberhymnal.org/htm/c/o/comeytpc.htm
NOW THANK WE ALL OUR GOD
http://www.cyberhymnal.org/htm/n/o/nowthank.htm
GIVE THANKS
http://www.cyberhymnal.org/htm/g/i/givthank.htm
THANKS TO GOD
http://www.cyberhymnal.org/htm/t/h/thankstg.htm
SING TO THE LORD OF HARVEST
http://www.cyberhymnal.org/htm/s/t/sttlohar.htm
WE PLOW THE FIELDS
http://www.cyberhymnal.org/htm/w/e/p/weplowtf.htm

MANNERS AND MENUS: THOUGHTS ON THE FIRST HARVEST FESTIVAL
http://www.plimoth.org/Library/manners.htm
THANKSGIVING ON THE NET
http://www.holidays.net/thanksgiving/
THANKSGIVING DAY
http://kids.infoplease.lycos.com/ce6/society/A0848350.html
BUTTERBALL TURKEYS: RECIPES AND IDEAS
http://www.butterball.com
OCEAN SPRAY CRANBERRIES—RECIPES
http://www.oceanspray.com/recipes.htm
THE FIRST THANKSGIVING—FACTS AND FANCIES
http://www.plimoth.org/Library/Thanksgiving/firstT.htm
FIRST AMERICAN NATIONAL THANKSGIVING—1777
http://www.plimoth.org/Library/Thanksgiving/1777.htm
PRIMARY SOURCES FOR THE "FIRST THANKSGIVING"
http://www.plimoth.org/Library/Thanksgiving/thnksref.htm
WHO ATTENDED THE 1621 "FIRST THANKSGIVING?"
http://www.plimoth.org/Library/Thanksgiving/thnksatt.htm
A 17TH CENTURY HARVEST FEAST
http://www.plimoth.org/Library/Thanksgiving/17feast.htm

Thanksgiving

THANKSGIVING IN AMERICAN HISTORY
   http://www.plimoth.org/Library/Thanksgiving/th1.htm
FOREFATHERS' DAY
   http://plimoth.org/Library/forefath.htm
A "FIRST THANKSGIVING" DINNER FOR TODAY
   http://www.plimoth.org/Library/Thanksgiving/afirst.htm
ROAST MEATS (INSTRUCTIONS ON COOKING, 1615)
   http://www.plimoth.org/Library/Thanksgiving/mroasts.htm
NO POPCORN!
   http://www.plimoth.org/Library/Thanksgiving/nopopc.htm
JULIANA SMITH'S 1779 THANKSGIVING
(A GOOD TELLING OF THE TRADITIONAL THANKSGIVING)
   http://www.plimoth.org/Library/Thanksgiving/juliana.htm
CELEBRATE! HOLIDAYS IN THE U.S.A.
THANKSGIVING DAY (US EMBASSY SITE, STOCKHOLM)
   http://www.usis.usemb.se/Holidays/celebrate/thanksgi.html
PLYMOUTH COLONY—THE EARLY YEARS
   http://kids.infoplease.lycos.com/ce6/history/A0860438.html
THE PILGRIMS' 1621 THANKSGIVING
   http://members.aol.com/calebj/thanksgiving.html
GEORGE WASHINGTON'S 1789 THANKSGIVING PROCLAMATION
   http://www.night.net/thanksgiving/kwash-11.html
ABRAHAM LINCOLN'S THANKSGIVING PROCLAMATION
   http://showcase.netins.net/web/creative/lincoln/speeches/thanks.htm
JUST FOR FUN TURKEY PAGE FROM BUTTERBALL
(COLORING PAGES & GAMES)
   http://www.butterball.com/pages/bb_Journal.cfm?JID=19
THANKSGIVING IN AMERICAN HISTORY
   http://plimoth.org/Library/Thanksgiving/th1.htm

Some of Our Favorite Findings this Week

It can be helpful to keep track of some of the favorite things you have discovered this week. Use this page to record some of these things for later review and further study.

Books: _____

_____

People: _____

_____

Places: _____

_____

Cool Words: _____

_____

Family Connections: _____

_____

Family Project of the Week: _____

_____

Internet Sites: _____

_____

_____

_____

Some Notes of Our Own: _____

_____

_____

_____

Appendix

Plymouth Colony

Excerpted from American History Stories
by Mara L. Pratt © 1886

One stormy day in December, 1620, there sailed into Cape Cod harbor a strange little vessel named the *Mayflower*. On board this little craft were a hundred brave men and women, who had come from England in order to escape "religious persecution." These are rather large words for little folks; but I think it better for you to learn them just here, because they seem somehow to belong to these particular people. Why, you will understand later.

Now, it seems rather cruel to leave these wanderers out in the cold storm; but we must for a few moments, while we hurry over to England to learn what had happened there to send these men and women across the ocean at this stormy time of the year.

A CHAPTER OF ENGLISH HISTORY

Very likely you have heard of Queen Elizabeth, or Good Queen Bess, as her people used to call her.

Long before Elizabeth herself was ruler over England, her father, King Henry the Eighth, had a great quarrel with the Pope at Rome. The Pope, being the head of the Catholic Church, sent certain orders to King Henry.

All England at that time was Catholic and had always obeyed the Pope in every point.

But King Henry made up his mind that he would obey no one; and that he would be the head of the Church himself. So he announced to his subjects that no longer were they to pay any attention to the Pope's orders, but that they were to obey him instead.

This seemed a fearful thing to some of the people. They believed God would send some terrible punishment to them. Still there were very many people in England who were glad of the change, and who, therefore, took the king's side in the trouble that followed.

King Henry died before the people had all grown used to the change and left the throne to his son Edward, who believed as his father had.

Thanksgiving

Edward died very soon after he came into power, and his sister, Mary, took the throne. Now, Mary was an earnest Catholic, and, as you would suppose, began at once bringing back the priests, and doing everything in her power to restore the old religion.

It would take many pages to record the names of the men and women who suffered terrible deaths for rebelling against her orders. But we must remember that Mary believed she was doing right, and that in doing these terrible deeds she was advancing the glory of her Church.

Mary's reign came to an end at last, and Queen Elizabeth took the throne. But Elizabeth was as strong a Protestant as Mary had been a Catholic; and again, because of their religious opinions people were persecuted, as in the times of King Henry and Queen Mary.

PURITANS AND PILGRIMS

But you will begin to wonder what all this has to do with the men and women we left in Cape Cod harbor. As you will see, it has everything to do with it.

During all this trouble in England, there had been rising a class of people who believed neither in the Catholic Church nor in the English Church.

These people dressed very strangely and acted even more strangely. Now, it was the fashion in those days for gentlemen to wear their hair long, and to dress in very elegant clothes; but those people who had arisen, and who hated both the churches, dressed in the very plainest of clothes, wore their hair so short that they were nick-named "Round Heads," would not allow music in their churches, would not have the old church service, and, in short, would have nothing but the very barest and plainest of everything.

These people were called Puritans, and Round Heads, and many other names by the rest of the English people, who looked upon them as fools and lunatics.

You may be sure the Puritans, or Round Heads, did not have a very enjoyable time in England.

At last, a little band of them, unable to bear their persecution, went over into Holland. There they lived happily enough, only that they longed for a home of their own, where they could teach their own religion and make it the religion of the country.

Appendix

For this reason they went back to England, obtained permission to found a colony in the new world, and with their hearts full of hope and courage, started out—two vessels full—for the unknown land. One of these vessels was obliged to put back into port because it was found to be unseaworthy. Thus it was that the *Mayflower*, one of the two, came into Cape Cod harbor alone.

You will often hear these Puritans, who came first to America, spoken of as Pilgrims, or the Pilgrim Fathers. This was a name they gave to themselves because of their pilgrimages to Holland and to America in search of a home. Try to remember this—these plain, honest, God-fearing people were all called Puritans in England, while the few who wandered about and finally settled Plymouth were given the extra name of Pilgrims.

THE PILGRIMS IN AMERICA

Let us go back to Cape Cod harbor now and see what these Pilgrims have been doing all this time. It was one of those snowy, windy days which we, who live near the Atlantic coast, expect to have now and then in the wintertime. Not a pleasant sort of a day to spend on the ocean, even in the snuggest and warmest of vessels. Much less pleasant it must have been to these wanderers in their rudely built vessel, drifting about as they were at the mercy of the wind and tide.

The Pilgrims had intended to land much farther south, where it was pleasanter and warmer; but the storm had been so severe they lost all control over the *Mayflower*, and were obliged to make port wherever they could.

I am afraid they were not over-pleased when their vessel came into Cape Cod harbor; for there they found only a rocky, desolate shore awaiting them; and, as it was in the dead of winter, you can imagine how cold and bare it all looked. The trees were leafless, the ground was frozen, and the waters about the shores were covered with sheets of ice.

But they were a brave, sturdy band. Although they would have been glad to be welcomed by the pleasant warmth of the southern lands, as they left their weather-beaten vessel, still they bravely accepted what was before them, perfectly sure that they had been guided to this shore by Divine power.

Thanksgiving

THE LANDING OF THE PILGRIM FATHERS

The breaking waves dashed high
On a stern and rockbound coast,
And the woods, against a stormy sky,
Their giant branches tossed;
And the heavy night hung dark
The hills and waters o'er,
When a band of exiles moored their bark
On the wild New England shore.
Not as the conqueror comes,
They, the true-hearted came;
Not with the roll of stirring drums,
And the trumpet that sings of fame;
Not as the flying come,
In silence and in fear;
They shook the depths of the desert's gloom
With their hymns of lofty cheer.
Amidst the storm they sang,
Till the stars heard, and the sea;
And the sounding aisles of the dim woods rang
To the anthem of the free.
The ocean-eagle soared
From his nest by the white wave's foam,
And the rocking pines of the forest roared
This was their welcome home.
There were men with hoary hair
Amidst that pilgrim band;
Why had they come to wither there,
Away from their childhood's land?
There was woman's fearless eye,
Lit by her deep love's truth;
There was manhood's brow serenely high,
And the fiery heart of youth.
What sought they thus afar?
Bright jewels of the mine?
The wealth of seas? The spoils of war?
They sought a faith's pure shrine.
Ay, call it holy ground,
The land where first they trod;
They have left unstained what there they found,
Freedom to worship God!

—Mrs. Hemans

Appendix

THE PILGRIMS AT WORK

As soon as all had landed, they gathered together about that large rock at the water's edge, known now as Plymouth Rock, and kneeling down thanked God for their safe deliverance from the perils of the sea.

Then they went sturdily to work. These men were not idle, lazy good-for-nothings, as those colonists in Virginia had been. They did not need a John Smith to urge them to be industrious. They were all terribly in earnest. They had left their native land, and with their brave wives, had come over to this wilderness to build homes for themselves.

Can't you fancy their axes ringing in the still winter days, as they felled the trees for lumber with which to build their rude houses?

Can't you fancy the brave, tender-hearted wives and mothers working on bravely in the bitter cold of their odd, uncomfortable houses, washing, ironing, baking, brewing, pounding the corn, spinning the cloth, and making the homes comfortable, and even cheerful, in the thousand ways which only mothers and wives can understand?

And the little boys and girls, too. There weren't very many of them to be sure; but can't you fancy how bravely the children of such noble men and women would behave, how they would try to bear the cold and hunger without a tear, and would try in all their little ways to do their part toward helping their papas and mammas to build up their village?

And there was one little baby, too. A little, wee, wee, baby boy, who was born during the voyage from England to America. I am afraid this little baby didn't have all the beautiful little clothes and fine laces, the lovely little toilet basket, with its dainty combs and brushes and puffs and powders that the babies we see have. I shouldn't wonder if the little stranger was wrapped in very ordinary shawls and blankets, and that the mother was very thankful if she could keep him from the cold. Nevertheless, I suspect this little baby had a very warm welcome from all these sturdy, hard-working men and women. For there is one beautiful thing about babies; they themselves are always so sweet and loveable, that it is a very hard-hearted man or woman whose heart is not drawn just a little toward the little, innocent, helpless things. I imagine the little fellow was the pet of the whole colony. Can't you see the women coming every day to look in upon the new baby, and the men, each glad to stop and amuse the little one for a minute as they went to and fro; and the children all happy to be allowed to take care of him now and then? This baby, I imagine, put a great deal of warm feeling into these busy colonists.

They gave the baby a very funny name you will think. They called him Peregrine, which means wandering, because he was born while those people were wandering about, searching for a new home.

Should you ever visit the town of Plymouth, you will find there, in Pilgrim Hall, the very cradle in which little Peregrine's mother used to rock him so many, many years ago.

Thanksgiving

The Plymouth Colony

from A Junior Class History of the United States,
by John J. Anderson © 1894

1. **The Plymouth Company**—In 1606, King James granted to the London Company the land lying between the thirty-fourth and thirty-eighth parallels, called South Virginia, this being the southern part of the territory which the English claimed on account of the discoveries made by the Cabots. The northern portion, lying between the forty-first and the forty-fifth parallels, he granted to a company called the Plymouth Company.[1] This Company, in 1607, began to form a settlement at the mouth of the Kennebec River,[2] but misfortunes discouraged the settlers, the most of whom returned to England, and the others went to Jamestown, Virginia.

2. **Smith's Exploration**—After this, nothing was done till 1614, when Captain John Smith, having recovered from the injuries which he had received in Virginia, went on a voyage of trade and discovery to the region near Cape Cod. He explored the coast from the Cape as far as the Penobscot River, and called the whole region *New England.*[3]

3. **The Puritans**—There were at that time in England a large number of people who did not believe that it was right to worship God in the manner required by the laws of the country, and as they were very strict in their religious notions and mode of living, they were nick-named Puritans. But King James was determined that all should attend the parish churches as provided by law, and would not allow any of the people to choose their own ministers and places of worship, as many thought they had right to do.

4. The result was, these people were obliged to meet secretly, often at night, to worship as they thought right, and when discovered, they were punished, sometimes by imprisonment. At length some of them left their homes in England with their pastor, John Robinson, and lived for a time in Holland; but hearing of the newly-discovered land beyond the ocean, and thinking that in such a country they could live, and worship God, in entire freedom, they resolved to go there.

5. **Sailing of the Mayflower**—After much trouble, they obtained a grant from the London Company; and leaving their pastor, as many as could be provided with quarters in the ship left Holland in a vessel called the *Speedwell* and sailed to Southampton in England. There they

were joined by other Puritans in a vessel called the *Mayflower*; and the two ships soon set sail, but had not gone far when the *Speedwell* was found to need repairs, and they were compelled to return. At last, after putting back a second time and leaving the *Speedwell* at Plymouth, [England,] they set sail from that port in their only ship, the *Mayflower* (September 16, 1620).

6. The number of Pilgrims[4] was about one hundred men, women, and children.[5] The most noted among them were John Carver, whom they afterward chose as their first governor, William Brewster, their elder, Miles Standish, their military leader, William Bradford, and Edward Winslow. After a voyage of about two months, they reached the coast near Cape Cod, having been carried considerably north of the place at which they intended to land (November 19).[6]

7. **Exploration of the Country**—As it was late in the season, and they were exhausted by their long voyage, they determined to seek a landing place without further delay. They therefore sailed into Cape Cod Bay, and sent out a party in a small boat to select a place for their settlement. Some of these were sent inland, while the others cruised along the shore. It was a dismal country, being covered with pine forests; and the explorers only caught a distant glimpse of the natives, who fled from them. Once, however, they were attacked, but they soon dispersed the savages.[7] It was only after a month's search that they found a fit place for their settlement.

8. **Landing of the Pilgrims**—They selected a harbor which, on Smith's map, was called Plymouth; and they also called the place Plymouth.[8] They landed on the 21st of December, 1620,[9] having previously, in the cabin of the *Mayflower*, drawn up a body of laws which they made a solemn vow to obey. The character of the Pilgrims was well suited to such an undertaking. They were earnest and devoted men, ready to brave all dangers and endure any hardships in the performance of their duty and in defense of their religion.

9. **Their First Winter**—During the first winter their sufferings were dreadful. With no houses but the few rude log cabins, which they had hastily constructed, and which scarcely protected them from the intense cold, with a scanty supply of food, and enduring so much fatigue and hardship, it is no wonder that many should have perished. By spring, only about one-half of their number were living. Among

those who had died were Governor Carver and his wife. Their second governor was William Bradford.

10. **Treaties with the Indians**—At first they were in fear of the Indians, who were sometimes seen lurking in the woods, but fled as soon as the English approached them. One day, however, an Indian, to their surprise, boldly entered the settlement, and exclaimed, "Welcome, Englishmen!" This was a chief named Samoset, who had picked up a little knowledge of English among the fishermen on the coast of Maine. In a few days Massasoit (mas-s-soit'), the great chief of the Wam-pan-o'-ags, came with a number of his warriors to pay the strangers a friendly visit. The Pilgrims made a treaty with the chief, and afterward with Ca-non'-i-cus, the chief of the Nar-ra-gan'-setts.[10]

11. **Growth of the Plymouth Colony**—For some time the settlers suffered greatly for the want of provisions; and it was not until the lands were divided among the settlers that the Colony commenced to prosper.[11] Their numbers did not increase fast, for only good and pious men were desired to join them. Ten years after their settlement, they obtained a grant of the land which they occupied, from the Council of Plymouth, who had succeeded to the powers and rights of the Plymouth Company. The colony, at that time, numbered about three hundred persons.

12. As the Puritans were still persecuted in England, very many desired to seek freedom in the wilds of New England. Some of these obtained from the Council of Plymouth a grant of land lying north of the Plymouth colony, and bordering on Massachusetts Bay; and in 1628 a number of persons came out under John En'-di-cott, and settled at a place which they called Salem. Others soon followed, settling at Salem and Charlestown. This was the commencement of the Massachusetts Bay Colony, a charter being granted by Charles I, the following year (1629).

FOOTNOTES

[1] "This patent conveyed a grant of the land along the coast for fifty miles, on each side from the place of their first habitation, and extending one hundred miles into the interior." —Edward Everett

[2] "Captain George Popham was their president. They went to work building a fort, storehouse, dwellings, and even a vessel. She was called the *Virginia*, and her size was thirty tons. Her first voyage was made the next year to Virginia, and thence to England. Therefore the Kennebec River, which has since sent

Appendix

out so many vessels, has the honor of producing the first vessel built by English hands in America."

—Varney's *History of Maine*

[3] Smith published a "Description of New England," which was printed in 1616. This contains a very curious and interesting map of the country which he explored. On this map was the name of Plymouth. "On his return to England, Smith was permitted to present a copy of his map and of a Journal of his voyage to the king's second son, afterwards King Charles I, who, at his solicitation, gave names, principally of English towns, to some thirty points upon the coast." —Palfrey's *History*

[4] The Pilgrims, or Pilgrim Fathers, as they are often called, belonged to a sect of the Puritans called Independents, who believed in an entire separation from the Church of England. Others were opposed only to its ceremonies, mode of government, and form of prayers.

[5] One died during the voyage and one was born. "So there were just one hundred and one who sailed from Plymouth in England, and just as many arrived in Cape Cod harbor."

—Prince's *History of New England*

[6] "After they had discovered land, they were altogether ignorant where it was."

—Hubbard's *History of New England*

[7] "The following morning, at daylight, they had just ended their prayers, and were preparing breakfast at their camp on the beach, when they heard a yell, and a flight of arrows fell among them. The assailants turned out to be thirty or forty Indians, who, being fired upon, retired. Neither side had been harmed. A number of the arrows were picked up, 'some whereof were headed with brass, others with hart's horn, and others with eagle's claws.'" —Palfrey's *History of New England*

[8] "All landed at a place which they called Plymouth, in grateful remembrance of the last town they left in their native country." —Hannah Adam's *N.E. History (1799)*

[9] By the old style of reckoning it was December 11th. When the practice of celebrating the anniversary of the Pilgrims began, in 1769, eleven, instead of ten days were erroneously added to the recorded date, to accommodate it to the corrected calendar, adopted in England in 1752. This led to the custom of celebrating the anniversary on the 22nd day of December.

[10] At first, Canonicus was inclined to be hostile. He sent to Plymouth a bundle of arrows bound with a rattlesnake's skin, this being the Indian mode of declaring war. Governor Bradford filled the skin with powder and ball and sent it back. Canonicus took it for a fatal charm: and the superstitious Indians passed it from village to village, till it came back to Plymouth. They did not dare touch it.

[11] "In August, 1623, the colony of New Plymouth remained as yet very feeble. The best dish that would be set before the third supply of colonists, about sixty in number, was a lobster, a piece of fish, and a cup of 'fair spring water.' As to bread, there was none in the colony." —Hildreth

Thanksgiving

<u>Captain John Smith</u>

Excerpted from Harper's New Monthly Magazine
by Benson J. Lossing © November, 1860

. . .History has made no record of Captain Smith's career during four years after his return to England [after leaving Jamestown]. Doubtless his most brilliant hopes and fondest desires were centered on the New World. In confirmation of the opinion, we find him, in 1614, engaged in an expedition, in company with several London gentlemen, for trade and discovery on the coast of North Virginia, a way to which had recently been opened by Gosnold, Pring, and Weymouth. They had seen only its line of coast, the vast interior was yet an unknown land to the civilized world.

To that land, full of courage and hope, Captain Smith sailed in March, 1614, with two vessels, one of them commanded by Captain Thomas Hunt. They first touched the coast off Maine, and while the crews of the vessels were engaged in catching and preserving fish, during July and August, Smith, with eight men in a small boat, carefully examined and surveyed the whole coast from the Penebscot to Cape Cod. They trafficked and they fought with the Indians as circumstances required.

From the topographical materials he had gathered, Captain Smith was enabled to construct quite an accurate map, not only of the coast but of the interior county watered by the principal streams which he had explored. He placed the Indian names of places on his map, except those which he had given to particular localities; and after an absence of less than seven months, he returned to England, leaving one of his vessels in command of Hunt to traffic with the natives.

Hunt not only disobeyed orders, but committed one of the worst crimes known in the calendar of human infamy. As soon as Smith had departed he kidnapped twenty-seven Indians, with **Squanto** their chief, took them to Spain, and sold several of them for slaves. Some benevolent friars took the remainder to educate them as missionaries. Among these was **Chief Squanto**, who was afterward returned to his people.

On his return to England, Captain Smith presented his map to the eldest son of King James (afterward Charles the First), and desired him to substitute better titles to places that the "barbarous names" he had recorded. He had named the country thus delineated **New England**, and he asked the Prince to confirm the same. That portion of North Virginia was called New England, and many names in that region, which appeared on Smith's corrected map, are still retained.

Appendix
<u>The Origin of Thanksgiving</u>
from Good Things for Thanksgiving
by Marie Irish © 1912

Thanksgiving Day comes to us from the misty past, in the early days of history. Centuries before the birth of Christ the Israelites set apart days for Thanksgiving, and in the fall of the year for seven days they held the Feast of Tabernacles which was a thanksgiving for the completed harvests.

The Romans each autumn held Thanksgiving feasts in honor of Ceres, the goddess of fruits and grains; while the Greeks held similar festivals as a thanksgiving to Demeter, their goddess of agriculture.

Various nations have held days of thanksgiving when they gave thanks for deliverance from danger of affliction, or for some especial blessing. The Dutch held such a Thanksgiving in Leyden, in 1575, after relief from the siege by the Spaniards. England, in 1588, appointed a day of Thanksgiving for the defeat of the Spanish Armada. Another English Thanksgiving day was held in February, 1872, to give thanks for the restoration to health of the Prince of Wales.

But an annual national Thanksgiving Day is a custom distinctly American and is observed by no other nation in the world. It originated with the Pilgrims of Plymouth Colony in November of 1621 a little less than a year after their landing in New England. It was a day appointed for religious purposes, that the settlers might have an oppor- tunity to express their gratitude for the perils they had passed, and for the blessings they were enjoying.

The first year in the new country had been a long, hard one; their only neighbors were savages, though these fortunately were friendly. The land was practically a wilderness and the comforts of the old home were lacking; but they had escaped the persecution of the Church of England, and were free to worship in their own way and according to their own consciences. It had been a year of hard work, but the field had produced enough to support them during the coming winter, and their houses were strong and warmly built.

Accordingly, a day was set apart by Governor Bradford to mark the beginning of a season of prayer and gratitude. The ceremonies lasted for several days and were attended by the Indian king, Massasoit, and ninety of his band. It was not intended at that time to make this a year- ly custom. Two years later, when rains came after a season of drought, another day of thanksgiving was held. Then again, three days later, when relief from famine came from England, the gratitude of the colonists was expressed in a Thanksgiving Day, and after that the custom was usually observed annually.

Later the colonies of New England, and in New York and Pennsylvania, adopted the Thanksgiving festival, and when George Washington made his first Thanksgiving Day proclamation, it was taken up all over the country. Washington chose the last Thursday in November, but for some years there was no regular date for celebration, it occurring some time during the autumn.

The present custom of a national Thanksgiving on the last Thursday of each November is probably due to Mrs. Sarah Hale, who wrote the governors of the various states regarding it, and finally suggested to President Lincoln that he issue such a proclamation. Since President Lincoln's proclamation in 1863, naming the last Thursday of November as the day for National Thanksgiving, that day has been regularly observed.

Gran'ther Baldwin's Thanksgiving

by Horatio Alger, Jr. © 1875

UNDERNEATH protected branches, from the highway just aloof;
Stands the house of Grand'ther Baldwin, with its gently sloping roof.
Square of shape and solid-timbered, it was standing, I have heard,
In the days of Whig and Tory, under royal George the Third.
Many a time, I well remember, I have gazed with childish awe
At the bullet-hole remaining in the sturdy oaken door,
Turning round half-apprehensive (recking not how time had fled)
Of the lurking, savage foeman from whose musket it was sped.
Not far off, the barn, plethoric with the autumn's harvest spoils,
Holds the farmer's well-earned trophies—the guerdon of his toils;
Filled the lofts with hay, sweet-scented, ravished from the meadows green,
While beneath are stalled the cattle, with their quiet, drowsy mien.
Deep and spacious are the grain-bins, brimming o'er with nature's gold;
Here are piles of yellow pumpkins on the barn-floor loosely rolled.
Just below in deep recesses, safe from wintry frost chill,
There are heaps of ruddy apples from the orchard on the hill.
Many a year has Grand'ther Baldwin in the old house dwelt in peace,
As his hair each year grew whiter, he has seen his herds increase.

Appendix

Sturdy sons and comely daughters, growing up from childish plays,
One by one have met life's duties, and gone forth their several ways.
Hushed the voice of childish laughter, hushed is childhood's merry tone,
the fireside Grand'ther Baldwin and his good wife sit alone.
Turning round half-apprehensive (recking not how time had fled)
Of the lurking savage foeman from whose musket it was sped.
Not far off, the barn, plethoric with the autumn harvest spoils,
Holds the farmer's well-earned trophies—the guerdon of his toils;
Filled the lofts with hay, sweet-scented, ravished from the meadows green,
While beneath are stalled the cattle, with their quiet drowsy mien.
Deep and spacious are the grain-bins, brimming o'er with nature's gold;
Here are piles of yellow pumpkins on the barn-floor loosely rolled.
Just below in deep recesses, safe from wintry frost and chill,
There are heaps of ruddy apples from the orchard on the hill.
Many a year has Grand'ther Baldwin in the old house dwelt in peace,
As his hair each year grew whiter, he has seen his herds increase.
Sturdy sons and comely daughters, growing up from childish plays,
One by one have met life's duties, and gone forth their several ways.
Hushed the voice of childish laughter, hushed is childhood's merry tone,
By the fireside Grand'ther Baldwin and his good wife sit alone.
Yet once within the twelvemonth, when the days are short and drear,
And chill winds chant the requiem of the slowly fading year,
When the autumn work is over, and the harvest gathered in,
Once again the old house echoes to a long unwonted din.
Logs of hickory blaze and crackle in the fireplace huge anti-high,
Curling wreaths of smoke mount upward to the gray November sky.
Ruddy lads and smiling lasses, just let loose from schooldom's cares,
Patter, patter, race and clatter, up and down the great hall stairs.
All the boys shall hold high revel; all the girls shall have their way,-
That's the law at Grand'ther Baldwin's upon each Thanksgiving Day.
From the parlor's sacred precincts, hark! a madder uproar yet;
Roguish Charlie's playing stage-coach, and the stage-coach has upset!
Joe, black-eyed and laughter-loving, Grand'ther's specs his nose across,
Gravely winks at brother Willie, who is gayly playing horse.
Grandma's face is fairly radiant; Grand'ther knows not how to frown,
though the children, in their frolic, turn the old house upside down.
For the boys may hold high revel, and the girls must have their way;
That's the law at Grand'ther Baldwin's upon each Thanksgiving Day.

Thanksgiving

But the dinner—ah! the dinner—words are feeble to portray
What a culinary triumph is achieved Thanksgiving Day!
Fairly groans the board with dainties, but the turkey rules the roast,
Aldermanic at the outset, at the last a fleshless ghost.
Then the richness of the pudding, and the flavor of the pie,
When you've dined at Grandma Baldwin's you will know as well as I.
When, at length, the feast was ended, Grand'ther Baldwin bent his head,
And, amid the solemn silence, with a reverent voice, he said:—
"Now unto God, the Gracious One, we thanks and homage pay,
Who guardeth us, and guideth us, and loveth us always!
"He scatters blessings in our paths, He giveth us increase,
He crowns us with His kindnesses, and granteth us His peace.
"Unto himself, our wandering feet, we pray that He may draw,
And may we strive, with faithful hearts, to keep His holy law!"
His simple words in silence died: a moment's hush. And then
From all the listening hearts there rose a solemn-voiced Amen!

Song—for November

While skies glint bright with bluest light
Through clouds that race o'er field and town,
And leaves go dancing left and right,
And orchard apples tumble down;
While school-girls sweet, in lane or street,
Lean 'gainst the wind and feel and hear
Its glad heart like a lover's beat—
So reigns the rapture of the year.
Then ho! And hey! And whoop-hooray!
Though winter clouds be looming,
Remember a November day
Is merrier than mildest May
With all her blossoms blooming.
While birds in scattered flight are blown
Aloft and lost in bosky mist,
And truant boys scud home alone
'Neath skies of gold and amethyst;
While twilight falls, and echo calls
Across the haunted atmosphere,
With low, sweet laughs at intervals—
So reigns the rapture of the year.

Appendix

Then ho! And hey! And whoop-hooray!
Though winter clouds be looming,
Remember a November day
Is merrier than mildest May
With all her blossoms blooming.

—James Whitcomb Riley

A Thanksgiving Hymn

For bud and for bloom and for balm-laden breeze,
For the singing of birds from the hills to the seas,
For the beauty of dawn and the brightness of noon,
For the light in the night of the stars and the moon,
We praise thee, gracious God.
For the sun-ripened fruit and the billowy grain,
For the orange and apple, the corn and the cane,
For the bountiful harvests now gathered and stored,
That by thee in the lap of the nations were poured,
We praise thee, gracious God.
For the blessings of friends, for the old and the new,
For the hearts that are trusted and trusting and true,
For the tones that we love, for the light of the eye
That warms with a welcome and glooms with good-bye,
We praise thee, gracious God.
That the desolate poor may find shelter and bread,
That the sick may be comforted, nourished, and fed,
That the sorrow may cease of the sighing and sad,
That the spirit bowed down may be lifted and glad,
We pray thee, pitying Lord.
That brother the hand of his brother may clasp
From ocean to ocean in friendliest grasp,
That for north and for south and for east and for west,
The horror of war be forever at rest,
We pray thee, pitying Lord.
For the blessings of earth and of air and of sky,
That fall on us all from the Father on high,
For the crown of all blessing since blessing begun,
For the gift, "the unspeakable gift," of thy Son,
We praise thee, gracious God.

—S.E. Adams

81

Thanksgiving

Remembering God with Thanksgiving

The art of thanksgiving is thanksliving.
It is gratitude in action.
It is applying Albert Schweitzer's philosophy:
"In gratitude for your own good fortune you must render in return some
sacrifice of your life for other life."
It is thanking God for the gift of life by living it triumphantly.
It is thanking God for your talents and abilities by accepting them as
obligations to be invested for the common good.
It is thanking God for all that men and women have done
for you by doing things for others.
It is thanking God for opportunities by accepting them
as a challenge to achievement.
It is thanking God for happiness by striving to make others happy.
It is thanking God for beauty by helping to make
the world more beautiful.
It is thanking God for inspiration by trying to be
an inspiration for others.
It is thanking God for health and strength by the care and
reverence you show your body.
It is thanking God for the creative ideas that enrich
life by adding your own
creative contributions to human progress.
It is thanking God for each new day by living it to the fullest.
It is thanking God by giving hands, arms, legs, and voice
to your thankful spirit.
It is adding to your prayers of thanksgiving, acts of thanksliving.

—Wilferd A. Peterson

Appendix

Evening

from Prayers at Vailima, by Robert Louis Stevenson

We come before Thee, O Lord, in the end of thy day with thanksgiving.

Our beloved in the far parts of the earth, those who are now beginning the labours of the day what time we end them, and those with whom the sun now stands at the point of noon, bless, help, console, and prosper them.

Our guard is relieved, the service of the day is over, and the hour come to rest. We resign into thy hands our sleeping bodies, our cold hearths, and open doors. Give us to awake with smiles, give us to labour smiling. As the sun returns in the east, so let our patience be renewed with dawn; as the sun lightens the world, so let our loving-kindness make bright this house of our habitation.

Various Prayers

Thou that has given so much to me,
Give one thing more—a grateful heart;
Not thankful when it pleases me,
As if Thy blessings had spare days;
But such a heart, whose pulse may be
Thy praise.
—George Herbert

Oh, Lord, I thank you for the privilege and gift of living in a world filled with beauty and excitement and variety.

I thank you for the gift of loving and being loved, for the friendliness and understanding and beauty of the animals on the farm and in the forest and marshes, for the green of the trees, the sound of the waterfall, the darting beauty of the trout in the brook.

I thank you for the delights of music and children, of other people's thoughts and conversation, and their books to read by the fireside or in bed with the rain falling on the roof or the snow blowing past outside the window.

—Louis Bromfield

Thanksgiving

The unthankful heart . . . discovers no mercies; but let the thankful heart sweep through the day and, as the magnet finds the iron, so it will find, in every hour, some heavenly blessings!

—Henry Ward Beecher

Thankfulness is a way of worshiping. All through the Psalms the emphasis is on thankfulness: "Sing to the Lord with thanksgiving" . . . "Let us come before His presence with thanksgiving" . . . "O give thanks unto the Lord, for He is good; for His steadfast love endures forever" . . . "I will give thanks to the Lord with my whole heart."

When Jesus healed the ten lepers only one returned to fall at the feet of the Master and give thanks to God. With this in mind someone has written that nine were healed, while the one who gave thanks was made whole. The expression of gratitude made the big difference.

Creative gratitude is a force for harmony and goodwill. It brings people together in love and understanding. It is high on the scale of creative qualities to be practiced day in and day out in our moment-to-moment contacts.

—Wilferd A. Peterson

Founded On . . .

It cannot be emphasized too strongly or too often that this great nation was founded, not by religionists, but by Christians; not on religions, but on the gospel of Jesus Christ! For this very reason, peoples of other faiths have been afforded asylum, prosperity, and freedom to worship here.

—Patrick Henry